The 50 Most Romantic Things Ever Done

DINI VON MUEFFLING

GROVE PRESS

New York

How do I love thee? Let me count the ways.

—ELIZABETH BARRETT BROWNING

The 50 Most Romantic Things Ever Done

The Man Across the Aisle

Jane L. was flying from New York to Washington on business. As she sat on the shuttle, she noticed a well-dressed, handsome man across the aisle from her, reading the newspaper. There was something about the man that made Jane incapable of taking her eyes off him. During the flight, she kept looking over at him, and soon he was glancing back at her. Crazy as it may have seemed, even though she hadn't spoken to him, she found herself thinking, "That's the man I'm going to marry." When they got off the plane, they continued to glance in each others' direction, but were too shy to speak.

At the taxi stand, Jane stood ahead of her mystery man. Time was quickly running out and she began to worry. She was next in line; the cab arrived, and with one look back she got in. As it began to pull away, she looked out the window and saw the man running after her car. "Stop," she cried out to the driver, but by then they had pulled too far out into the quick-moving traffic. Jane looked out the back window; as they drew farther and faster away, she could see the man was waving madly to her. Quickly, she reached into her bag and scrawled her number on a piece of paper, pressing it against the cab's rear window. But he was too far away to read it.

A short time later, while at her business meeting, a

distressed Jane could not focus on work, thinking only that she had seen the man she was going to marry and then had lost him. It was unbearable. Feigning illness, she bolted from the meeting and headed back to the airport.

"Of course!" she realized. "He had no baggage! He'll be returning to New York today too."

Jane sat in the shuttle departure area at National, waiting. Every hour she scanned the passengers boarding the shuttle, but there was no sign of him. By the last flight at nine she was at a loss for what else to do, so she reluctantly got on the plane back to New York. During the flight, her mind raced back and forth, alternating between figuring out how she was going to try to find him and thinking that she must be insane to have behaved so rashly. At the sight of Manhattan's skyscrapers, she realized her cause was lost. She debarked from the shuttle for the second time that day, only now with dejection. Stepping into the gate area, she looked ahead. And there he was.

"What took you so long?" he asked. "I've been waiting all day."

Love Notes

There is no greater romantic gesture that an artist can make than to be inspired by and create for his love. Such was the gift that the great composer Richard Wagner presented to his wife, Cosima, on the occasion of her thirty-third birthday, on Christmas Day in 1870.

Cosima was the daughter of the pianist and composer Franz Liszt, the nineteenth century's greatest musical idol. The young Cosima, who was pretty and clever, was educated in musical instruction by one of her father's pupils and acolytes, a famous pianist and conductor, Hans von Bulow. Von Bulow was smitten by Cosima, who in turn was flattered by his attention and accepted his proposal of marriage.

The marriage turned out to be a passionless one, however, and Cosima soon discovered that all of Hans's energy went into his music. They remained a couple nonetheless, and in 1858 they visited Wagner in Zurich at the home of a wealthy banking family who were admirers of his. Wagner was already famous as a composer and as a radical thinker. Like Franz Liszt, he was a notorious womanizer, carrying on an affair with his host's wife at the time, although he was married.

Wagner was also writing the poem and a portion of the music to his most sensual opera, *Tristan und Isolde*, based on the legendary love story. *Tristan*'s libretto was read by Cosima, who found herself profoundly disturbed by the feelings it stirred in her. She also found herself falling in love with the composer, with whom the von Bulows had become close friends. Five years later, Wagner came to Berlin to visit the von Bulows, and his and Cosima's long-simmering attraction for each other blossomed. They became lovers.

Over the next half decade, their relationship became the music world's most notorious open secret. Wagner became a widower when his wife died in 1866, but Cosima was still married and the mother of two children. Von Bulow seemed not to have cared about the affair, which he must have known about; rather, he was devoted to Wagner's music, even conducting the premier of *Tristan und Isolde*. During this time Cosima gave birth to two more daughters, Isolde and Eva, this time by Wagner.

Wagner took up residence in a villa called "Triebschen," near Lucerne in Switzerland. Cosima finally reconciled her situation. She left von Bulow and took up "officially" with Wagner. The two married in 1868 and resided in Triebschen.

On Christmas morning of 1870, Wagner presented her with the most beautiful gift he could give her. Cosima described the scene in her diary:

> When I awoke I heard a sound, swelling ever more, until I could no longer believe I was dreaming. Music sounded, and what music! When it stopped, R. came to me with the five children and handed me the score of the *Symphonic Birthday Greetings*. I dissolved in tears. Everybody wept. R. had placed his orchestra on the staircase and sanctified our Triebschen forever.

After the family—and an astonished Nietzsche, who was visiting—ate breakfast, Wagner raised his baton again. This time the orchestra played Lohengrin's bridal march, the *Septet* of Beethoven, and then, once again, the *Triebschen Idyll*, as the piece of music had been named. Although the piece was meant to remain private, Wagner later used themes from it in his opera *Siegfried*. For this reason, and also to commemorate the birth of their son Siegfried the year before, the title was then changed to *Siegfried Idyll*. Cosima regretted that the beautiful composition was no longer solely hers, but hoped she would be compensated by the enjoyment others would have in hearing it.

Some years later, Cosima and Wagner moved to Bayreuth, where they established the Wagner Festival, and remained together until his death. Fiercely loyal to her great love, she continued to run the festival until she died in 1930.

It Happened One Night

The marriage of Clark Gable and Carole Lombard was a Hollywood anomaly simply because it was the genuine article. Over the four years that Tinseltown's reigning stars were together, they were never apart for more than a week. With Lombard, Gable was truly in love for the first time in his life, and he always made sure she knew it. Their years together were marked by wonderfully romantic—and, typically for Carole—screwball gestures of their love.

Though they had made a film together in 1932, Gable and Lombard had thought little of each other at the time. Gable's interest in Lombard was not piqued until he saw her at the White Mayfair Ball in Hollywood, which she was chairing in January 1936. The dress code for the women was white gowns, and Carole's shimmering satin sheath clung to her like a second skin. As hostess of the evening, she hardly had a moment for her former costar. But when Gable, gorgeous in his white tie and tails, approached as the orchestra struck up "Cheek to Cheek," she looked at him quizzically. He seemed nervous as he said, grinning, "I go for you, Ma," his nickname for her during filming. She realized he was asking her to dance and replied with considerably less enthusiasm, "I go for you, too, Pa."

They danced several times and then Gable asked her to come for a drive in his new sixteen-thousand-dollar Duesenberg convertible. Lombard was reluctant to leave the party, but eventually agreed when he seemed hurt. After a short while, she insisted that she needed to return. Angered that she wouldn't accompany him to his hotel for a drink, Gable careened back to the party. Matters were made worse when he begged off the after-party party that Lombard was throwing at her house, saying he had a prior appointment. Lombard sarcastically quipped it must be with another actress with whom he was rumored to be involved. The furious Gable went home to the Beverly Wilshire to drown his sorrows.

He awoke the next morning to find a white dove cooing on his chest. Thinking he must have the mother of all hangovers, he closed his eyes, then opened them again. The bird was still there and a second one was perched on the chandelier. A note attached to the leg of one of the doves revealed all: "How about it? Carole." Clark was delighted. Not only was this a peace offering, but he sensed that perhaps she liked him, too. He called to thank her, in the process mentioning that his place was beginning to smell a bit, so Lombard offered to keep the birds at her house. He could have visiting rights every Sunday afternoon, she added. Gable jumped at the chance to bring the pair of doves right to her, but she said she would send her butler instead.

As Gable's courtship intensified over the next month,

Lombard realized she was falling for him. She decided to find him a fabulous Valentine's Day present. Knowing that he had a passion for sports cars and that he was annoyed that Gary Cooper had bought the exact same Duesenberg he had, she decided to get him a car that no one else would own. At a junk yard she bought a broken-down Model T for fifteen dollars. She had it painted white with red hearts all over it, and then had it delivered to the MGM set of Gable's current movie. Although there was a note on the steering wheel that read, "You're driving me crazy," Gable didn't need a note to know who it was from. He called her up to invite her to go dancing with him that evening. It would be their first official date.

Wanting to look stunning, Carole put on a beaded champagne-colored gown, which she had worn in one of her movies. She imagined they would look dazzling as they drove through Hollywood in his fancy car. Gable had another plan. When he arrived at her house he was driving the shabby jalopy, which was barely running. With the joke on her, Lombard threw on a white chinchilla and hopped in as if she hadn't a care. They sputtered and creeped their way to the Cafe Trocadero, where they hit the dance floor to the song "You Were Meant for Me." Carole whispered to Clark, "They're playing our song." He agreed.

After a three-year courtship, they married. Lombard wanted to be sure that for the twice-married Gable, she was not just another feather in his cap. She wasn't. Theirs was one of the happiest Hollywood marriages. After their wedding, Lombard decided only to work when Gable worked, so they could share their time off for such un-glamorous passions as camping out, fishing, hunting, and relaxing at their ranch. When World War II began, Gable spearheaded the Hollywood effort to support his country. This included encouraging Americans to buy war bonds, and he asked his eager wife to lead the effort in her home state of Indiana. On January 15, 1942, Carole signed autographs in the Indianapolis State House for twelve hours, raising over two million dollars. At the day's close, she was pining to go home to Clark, with whom she had quarreled before leaving. She insisted in canceling her next stops and took the first plane available. Waiting back at the ranch, Gable had decorated the house with red, white, and blue streamers and had arranged a surprise dinner party for her. There were bouquets of red roses in every room and Gable ordered that the house be lit only by candles. They were never to see each other again. Lombard's plane made an unscheduled stop and then crashed shortly thereafter, killing everyone on board. Gable sped to Las Vegas to join the futile search for survivors, but was turned back. As he waited for a glimmer of hope that was never to come, a member of the search party brought him back the ruby and diamond earrings Lombard had been wearing, which he had given her for Christmas. Gable was destroyed with grief.

Although Gable married twice more, when he died, his last wife knew exactly where to lay him to rest: next to Lombard.

In Love and War

No two people have more exemplified the tragedy of the
civil war in Bosnia than twenty-five-year-old sweethearts
Bosko Brckic and Admira Ismic. The only impediment to
their love was living in a country whose people are divided solely on the basis of ethnic heritage. For Bosko, a
Serb, and Admira, a Muslim, the love they once expressed
openly for each other was forced to become secret.

The couple, who had been dating for seven years,
since high school, were both chemistry students at the
university in Sarajevo. Bosko remained in the city to be
with Admira despite his family's flight from the blood-
shed. Finally, in the spring of 1993, Admira chose to re-
ward Bosko for staying behind by fleeing Sarajevo with
him to Serb territory.

They knew their escape would be a dangerous one.
To get to the Serb side they had to cross the Vrbanja
Bridge, the front line between the Bosnian Serb and Muslim forces. While most who wished to flee the city dared
not risk the sniper fire, some had successfully crossed
over. On the day of their planned escape, carrying two
bags, Bosko and Admira approached the government
soldiers on the Bosnian side of the no-man's-land. They
asked the soldiers to let them try to escape, and the police
snipers assented.

The young lovers began running as fast as they could
across the bridge. They had almost reached the Serb side

when a Serb sniper opened fire. The machine gun fire came so rapidly that the couple had no chance to seek cover. Bosko was killed instantly, his body lying twisted on the ground. Mortally wounded, Admira crawled the few feet to her lover and wrapped her arm around him before she died.

In an ironic twist to the story of two people whose love transcended a country's war, both the Serbs and Muslims staked claims to the bodies. As the two sides argued about who would have them, Bosko and Admira's bodies lay intertwined on the bridge.

"The world must know about this," said Bosko's mother, Radmila, from the Serb side. "This cannot last forever, the Muslims and the Serbs. They cannot fight forever."

Radmila gave permission to Admira's father to bury her son's body on the Muslim side. She had but one stipulation. "I don't want them separated," she said.

"How Do I Love Thee?"

When the reclusive nineteenth-century poet Elizabeth Barrett praised the work of fellow poet Robert Browning in a poem she wrote, her intentions were merely to get him to correspond with her. Instead he sought her out and coaxed her from a reclusive life into one filled with passion.

Forty-year-old Elizabeth Barrett was one of Britain's foremost women poets. An invalid since adolescence, her illnesses and her overbearing widower father kept Elizabeth contained to her home. From an early age her only refuge was reading and, later, writing. But she also had a dread of meeting anyone outside her family.

Barrett had long admired the work of Robert Browning, whom she considered much underappreciated. She devised to get his attention by mentioning him in a poem, with the hopes that he would be flattered and respond. "Lady Geraldine's Courtship," published in 1844, was a long ballad about a romance between a noble woman and her lover Bertram, a "lowly" poet, in which Barrett generously praised Browning by name.

Although Browning was away in Italy when "Lady Geraldine's Courtship" was published, his sister sent him a copy, which he read. About six months later, he wrote to Barrett an immensely flattering and impassioned letter about her work. Elizabeth was beside herself with happiness. She felt she had found her soul mate—the one person with whom she could feel unbridled passion about poetry and other lofty matters. She viewed her feelings for Browning as of the highest spiritual level, nothing more, and asked him to honestly criticize her work and teach her. They began a correspondence and nearly immediately Browning asked to meet her. After putting him off as much as possible, Elizabeth realized a meeting was inevitable. She fixed an exact hour at which he was to come to the Barrett house, suggesting that if he missed the appointment, his chance would be blown. Browning was there.

The rapport they felt with each other in that first hour was undeniable. In his next letter to Elizabeth, Robert asked her to marry him. For the socially inept Barrett, her response was shock that he would mock her with such a suggestion; she had assumed that he was joking. Browning realized he needed to tread gently and slowly to make progress with her, and began again to correspond with her. For Elizabeth, this was the kind of friendship she had been dreaming of her whole life. She poured out her soul to Robert, and also wrote him a series of sonnets that she kept secret from him.

Finally Robert insisted that she face reality. They were in love and he wanted them to be together. Elizabeth swore that it was impossible and that she could never leave her father. After much tearful debate, Elizabeth decided she needed to live her life. She and Robert eloped to Italy, where they would be able to live well on little money.

For the first time in her life, Elizabeth discovered the meaning of love accompanied by passion. Her marriage changed her overnight, and although her health was still poor, she began to embrace life to the fullest. Robert worried endlessly about her, but Elizabeth thrived as a result of their passion. At the age of forty-two, she gave birth to a son, named Pen. She continued to write in Italy and she published to even further acclaim, although for her success had now become secondary to her marriage. When Robert's mother died just nine days after Pen's birth, Robert fell into an enormous depression. Barrett lifted his spirits by presenting him with the forty-three love sonnets she had written during their courtship. By 1859, however, Elizabeth's body began to fail her. She accepted the future and was happy knowing that she would leave behind what she had always assumed was impossible for her, a husband and a child of her own. On June 29, 1861, she died in her beloved Robert's arms.

Browning tried to shake off his grief by writing. In 1864, his *Dramatis Personae* was published to huge acclaim. As Elizabeth had predicted, Robert had finally attained the recognition she knew he deserved.

A Dream of a Proposal

When the actor Billy Baldwin proposed to his girlfriend, the singer Chynna Phillips, he worked hard to make it as romantic and memorable as possible.

Billy rented a suite at the elegant Carlyle Hotel in New York. The hotel has among its stores the Vera Wang Bridal Shop, whose wedding dresses are among the most beautiful in the world, confections of organza, tulle, and taffeta. Wang, a former figure skater, designed Nancy Kerrigan's graceful costumes for the Olympics, and regularly attires Billy's former *Sliver* costar, Sharon Stone.

Billy filled the suite with forty wedding dresses borrowed from Wang's shop, draping them over chairs and on the bed so that everywhere Chynna looked she would see a white dress. Then he also had the rooms filled with forty bouquets of white roses and put a magnificent diamond ring in his pocket. When Chynna entered the suite she was speechless. Fortunately, Billy knew exactly what he was going to say. And Chynna said yes.

Rumor has it they spent the rest of the weekend ordering room service, and Chynna probably trying on dresses. Nine months later, they had an all-white wedding.

Chynna wore a white organza Vera Wang dress, and to match his wife's bouquet, Billy sported a white rose in his lapel.

How He Got Her Name in the Paper

Celebrity publicists make their living by getting favorable press for their clients. It's a cutthroat, competitive business: They must promise big exclusives to columnists so that later they may request mentions of their other clients in the paper. In New York City, there are hundreds of publicists for thousands of clients, who all want to read flattering "items" about themselves.

Leslie S. was a publicist at PMK, one of the largest and most established public relations firms, and her clients included several television stars. One Sunday, she and her boyfriend, Cory Z., were reading the papers over breakfast. She had just moved in with Cory the day before and thought they might be getting engaged, but he hadn't popped the question. "Great," she thought. "We're living in sin."

She had finished reading the wedding announcements in the *New York Times*, as she did first every Sunday morning, and asked Cory for the *Daily News*, which he had been reading. Giving it to her, Cory said, "Benza is writing about your clients in his column, and your name is in there, too."

Leslie was confused. A. J. Benza's Sunday "Downtown" column chronicles the comings and goings of celebrities in New York nightlife. A true Italian New Yawka, Benza calls all women "doll" or "babe" and is tough about what he will put in his column. But Leslie hadn't pitched any items to him for his column, so she was surprised to read the following:

POP THE QUESTION
Leslie S., the PMK publicist, just landed a new client. She'll now be handling real estate executive Cory Z. If, that is, she accepts his marriage proposal, which he asked me to make for him. Which I just did right now. Cory and Leslie have been dating for six months. He says he and Leslie enjoy the column with coffee in bed. It took a lot of chutzpah to ask and that's why I agreed to it. It's the last time though. So all you romantics can come up with another idea.

Leslie put down the paper to find Cory down on one knee with a ring in his hand. And, of course, she said yes.

Arabian Nights

As long as she could remember, Isabel Arundell knew she was destined to live a wandering life with a tall, dark, handsome man in the Far East. The only problem was that—as was customary in the nineteenth century for a young woman from London's upper classes—she was naturally expected to marry her social equal. The pale, dark-haired Isabel refused to deny herself her dream, even though she had no idea how it was to be fulfilled.

The year before the teenage Isabel and her sisters were to make their debuts into society—effectively pronouncing their availability for marriage—the Arundell family lived in the English countryside, in Essex. There Isabel discovered gypsy encampments and befriended a young gypsy woman named Hagar Burton. Isabel listened for hours to Hagar's romantic tales of the nomadic life and would go home each night to devour books about the East. At the close of the year, before the family was to return to London, Hagar told Isabel her fortune:

> You will cross the sea, and be in the same town with your destiny and know it not. Every obstacle will rise up against you, and such a combination of circumstances that it will require all your courage, energy, and intelligence to meet them . . . . You will bear the name of our tribe, and be right proud of it. You will be as we are, but far greater than we. Your life is all wandering, changes, and adventure. One soul in two bodies in life or death, never long apart. Show this to the man you take for your husband.

Hagar promised a thrilled Isabel that it would come true and that the man she would marry would also be named Burton. After Isabel's debut, and after she turned down many proposals from eligible young men, the Arundells temporarily moved to the seaside resort town of Boulogne, France. Each day, Isabel and her sisters went for long walks along the ramparts for exercise. One day as they strolled, a man passed them who personified in appearance everything Isabel had dreamed for in her husband, including piercing dark eyes. He looked at her and she at him, and after he was gone she turned to her sisters and whispered, "That man will marry me." When they passed each other again the next day, he stopped and scrawled on a nearby wall with a piece of chalk, "May I speak to you?" Isabel wrote back, "No, Mother will be angry." A few weeks later, at a tea dance given by her cousin, Isabel saw her intended again. This time they were introduced: His name was Richard Burton. They danced several times and spoke at length, but, unfortunately for Isabel, Richard was leaving soon.

Richard Burton was the foremost Orientalist of his time, a wanderer who was British by birth but Eastern at heart. When he and Isabel met, Richard, sponsored by the Royal Geographical Society, was on his way to Mecca, which no white man had ever penetrated. If his true identity had been uncovered, he would have been killed on the spot. He had studied Arabic and the Muslim way of life extensively, and made his trip in disguise. After successfully completing the pilgrimage, he was awarded the green turban of the pious and named a hajji. His book on these experiences made him famous in England, and Isabel prayed that he would return to London to lecture. Instead he went back to Bombay.

Finally, after seven years away, he returned to London. Following their first meeting, Isabel had sworn that he was the only man for her, and much to her family's chagrin she would not be swayed. She followed his travels in the papers and dreamed of his return. By chance they met again, and this time Richard was smitten. He immediately proposed to Isabel, who, in an uncharacteristically weak moment, became concerned about going against her family. Richard left to journey to East Africa (from which no white man had ever returned alive), saying that he expected her answer upon his return.

Three long years later, after successfully making this trip, Richard demanded Isabel's reply. At thirty-one, she had waited a decade for him; she would not give him up now, and they eloped. Richard entered the Foreign Service and Isabel's life of wandering and devotion to her husband began at long last. Although they had many postings in exotic locales, Richard's "difficult" nature never garnered him the sort of superior position he was worthy of and had earned. Finally, they were posted in Damascus and the Burtons were ecstatic. Nowhere did they feel more at home, and at last Isabel was to live in her much dreamed-of East. She threw herself into learning Arabic, writing the consulate reports, and hosting visitors to the house.

It was not to last. A wanderer at heart, Richard was not the best diplomat, and Damascus was too important to England to leave in the hands of someone considered uncontrollable. When the position was taken from him, he went directly to Beirut, leaving Isabel to pack up. Hearing him calling for her in a dream, she ran to her stable, saddled a horse, and galloped for five hours through the night over rocks and through swamps to him. She made it to a coach stop and rode into Beirut, where she spied Burton walking up the street alone. He saw her and his face lit up. "Thank you," was all he said.

They lived out their lives in his next posting, Trieste, where Richard continued work on a project he had begun thirty years before, translating *A Thousand and One Nights*, also known as *The Arabian Nights*. When published, much to Isabel's and Richard's shock, his volumes were hailed as the most important translations ever done. He was an instant hero, the books bestsellers, and for the first time in their lives, the Burtons had money. Although in poor health, they continued to do what they loved most: travel. For their silver wedding anniversary came further news that England fully recognized their achievements: Richard was knighted. When Richard died several years later, Isabel took his body back to England and commissioned masons to fulfill his wish "to lie in an Arab tent." Made of Carrara marble, his resting place is fringed and gilded, topped by a golden nine-point star and a string of tinkling camel bells hung over the door. Isabel is buried by his side.

To Catch a Prince

Grace Kelly became America's first real princess when she married Prince Ranier of Monaco in 1956. Although the pairing of the beautiful movie star and the less-than-handsome monarch may have seemed odd to outsiders, it was very much a love match. Both Catholics who had lived much of their lives in the public eye, both were eager to settle down and have a family.

The couple met when Kelly was heading the American delegation to the Cannes Film Festival in 1955. She was already familiar with Monaco, having filmed Alfred Hitchcock's *To Catch a Thief* with Cary Grant there the year before. While her previous stay had been tainted by a failed romance with the fashion designer Oleg Cassini, professionally the actress was riding high from having just won the Academy Award as best actress for the film *The Country Girl*.

Grace's role as the head of the delegation was mainly titular, and her sole festival responsibility was a meeting with Monaco's ruler, Prince Ranier. It had been arranged by a journalist from the French magazine *Paris Match* and was intended to provide a nice photo opportunity. When Kelly confided to her then beau, the French actor Jean-Pierre Aumont, that she was going to cancel the meeting because it was an hour and a half away and didn't afford her enough time to make it to her hair appointment before an early-evening festival reception, Aumont was horrified. He explained to Grace that to cancel on the reigning prince—particularly for the paltry excuse that she wanted to get to the hairdresser—was just not done.

A reluctant Kelly went back to her room to prepare for the meeting. To her horror, she discovered when she plugged in her blow-dryer that it would not operate because there was an electrical strike in France. So too was the maid unable to iron any of Grace's clothes, and she was forced to wear her only unrumpled dress, which, with its dark background and huge flowers, looked like a bad sofa. When Grace got to the lobby, the *Match* journalist asked her where her hat was—it was necessary to wear one to the palace. She returned to her room and made a wreath of artificial flowers with which to crown her soaking hair.

The prince kept Kelly waiting for over an hour as he finished lunch at his Cap Ferrat villa with some guests. The much put-out Grace was even testier now. When Ranier finally arrived he offered to take her on a tour of the palace. She had spent the last hour doing just that, so the prince took her to his private zoo instead, at last making a favorable impression with his familiarity with the exotic animals. When he reached inside the tiger cage to stroke one of the big cats, Grace softened. She left the palace more cheerful than when she arrived.

Being well-mannered, Kelly sent the prince a thank-you note for hosting her at the palace. Delighted, he immediately wrote back. Her behavior countered everything he expected from the American film star, and soon they were corresponding regularly. Writing proved to Ranier's milieu; on the page he was wise, witty, and of an open heart and mind. Kelly had found a true friend in the long, beautiful letters written to her.

The American press had already heard rumors of a romance between the two, which Kelly vigorously denied. Not wanting to spoil her new friendship and the possibility of a romance, she said she had not heard from the prince since their first meeting. While she didn't like to lie, at twenty-six, having watched her childhood friends become wives and mothers, she wanted very much to get married.

As soon as filming on her new movie wrapped up, Grace packed madly to get home to Baltimore and the annual Kelly family Christmas party. Ranier, it turned out, would be attending.

This rather surprising turn of events was the result of a lot of convoluted behind-the-scenes arranging about which Grace knew nothing. Two close family friends of the Kellys, Aunt Edie and Uncle Russ Austin, had been in Monaco the previous summer and had found themselves confronted with a social dilemma. They had wanted to attend the Red Cross Ball, the most swank of the summer parties there, but all the tickets had been sold. Remembering that Grace had met with the prince in the spring, Uncle Russ audaciously called the palace to see if the prince could get them in. Ranier was only too happy to oblige and turned the task of delivering the tickets over to Father Francis Tucker, his priest. Ranier had already spoken with him about his feelings for Grace, and when the monarch made plans for a trip to the United States, ostensibly for the purpose of a medical checkup at Johns Hopkins Hospital, Father Tucker recommended to the Austins that they invite him to lunch. The Austins promised the prince they would bring him to the Kelly Christmas party afterward. A nervous Grace was uncertain about the whole endeavor, but the afternoon turned quickly into evening and it was clear that the prince was enjoying himself. Finally, at ten o'clock, Grace's mother suggested that perhaps the prince and his aide would want to spend the night in the guest bedrooms. Ranier leapt at the offer. The prince and Grace spent the next few days together, driving in the country and playing cards. Their happiness seemed so perfectly natural that after three days none of the Kellys was surprised when Grace announced she would become Ranier's wife.

Naturally, the announcement on January 5 sent the press into a frenzy. After completing her role in what would be her last feature film, *High Society*, Kelly spent a month hastily preparing for her wedding. With fifty friends and family members, she traveled across the Atlantic to Monaco on the *Constitution*. Her arrival into the harbor of Monaco was the grandest entrance a girl could have expected. As a flotilla of boats surrounded the ocean liner, Grace stepped out onto the gangplank that connected the ship with her fiancé's yacht. At that moment, hundreds of red and white carnations were dropped from a seaplane overhead, a gift from Aristotle Onassis. It seemed that all of Monaco had turned out to greet their new princess.

On August 19, 1956, in Monaco's hilltop cathedral, Grace Patricia accepted the charge offered her by the bishop to marry Ranier Louis Henri Maxence Betrand. The bride wore a dress created for her by the Hollywood costume designer Helen Rose, consisting of 150 yards of Valenciennes lace, silk, silk tulle, and taffeta. As much fabric as was involved, the dress looked simple and elegant and the bride stunning in it. The groom wore a military uniform he designed himself, decorated in gold leaf. After the bishop pronounced the couple man and wife, the prince and princess made one stop on their way to their honeymoon: the tiny chapel of St. Devota, the patron saint of Monaco, located in the port. There Grace knelt before the altar and laid her bridal bouquet upon it. She moved her lips, as if in prayer, and offered herself to her new home and people.

Take the F Train

There is one young New York City couple who is happy that crime hasn't been altogether wiped out in the Big Apple. One evening last year, Elizabeth F. boarded the Brooklyn-bound F train as she did every day after work. Settling onto her seat, she looked across the car at a young man. For inexplicable reasons, she says, "I felt this deep connection with him."

But before she had a chance to establish eye contact, Elizabeth was attacked by a mugger, who grabbed the heart locket she wore around her neck and ran. Stunned, she looked up to see the stranger from across the car dash out the closing doors of the train after the thief.

Elizabeth was distraught. She didn't care about the necklace—it had been a gift from her ex-boyfriend. She was worried about the gallant young man.

"I wondered if he was all right," she says. "Who was he? Was he thinking about me, too?"

Weeks passed, during which Elizabeth told the story to everyone she knew, mainly in the hopes that they might have heard her hero's version and know who he was. Unfortunately, but unsurprisingly, no one did.

Then several months later she was with some girl-friends at a local Brooklyn nightclub. The bartender called to her and handed her a glass of white wine, pointing to a man at the far end of the bar. Elizabeth glanced at the glass, and to her surprise, saw her necklace at the bottom of it. She then looked up to see her guardian angel standing in front of her.

"How did you get this?" she asked. "How did you find me here?"

"I grabbed it from the man who snatched it," said the man. "I carried it with me everywhere in the hopes that one day we would meet again."

Several months later he gave Elizabeth a new piece of jewelry: a wedding band.

The King and Mrs. Simpson

The most famous love story of this century is that of King Edward and Mrs. Simpson, for whom he gave up his throne in 1933. This gesture of love divided the people of Britain: While many citizens viewed the abdication as romantic and right, many others were shocked that Edward would abandon his duties for a twice-divorced American socialite. But the king let his heart lead the way.

Prince Edward was undoubtedly the world's most eligible bachelor. A great sportsman, he was slender and fit, had golden hair, pale blue eyes, and a healthy tan. He also had refined taste and dressed impeccably, setting the style of the time. He was also, however, quite spoiled, a heavy drinker, and carried on affairs with women, married and not, in the rarefied society circles in which he traveled. Implored by his parents to settle down and marry, the prince assured them that someday he would.

What so few understood about the prince was that he was like a child and needed to be treated accordingly. Wallis Simpson grasped this at their first meeting. She had moved to London with her second husband, Ernest, a partner in a global shipping company based on both sides of the Atlantic. Among their expatriate friends from America was Thelma Furness, twin sister of Gloria Vanderbilt and wife of the immensely rich Lord Furness. The stunning Thelma was also the prince's mistress. When the invitation was issued to the Simpsons to spend a weekend at Thelma's in the country and meet the prince, the social-climbing Wallis was ecstatic.

Wanting to make a lasting impression on the heir, Wallis was determined to say something to him that would force him to notice her. She watched him all evening in Thelma's house, and when he finally turned to speak to her, asking her if she didn't find English country houses drafty and cold, she rebuked him for his question, saying all English men asked that of American women and that she had expected something more original from the crown prince. Wallis had discovered his Achilles' heel: Edward loved to be challenged and dominated. He could not get her out of his mind.

Shortly thereafter Thelma left for the United States. As soon as she was gone, Edward's and Wallis's affair began in earnest.

Wallis began to reign as London society's leading lady. She and the prince were invited everywhere and consorted with not just the most important society people, but also writers, actors, artists, and politicians. They traveled together throughout Europe. In London, the prince shocked his family and others by accompanying Wallis to events such as Ascot and the Silver Jubilee Ball. He was defying all the rules for a royal's conduct and did not care. Then his father, the king, died in January 1936. Although Wallis was excluded from the funeral and accession ceremonies, by the prince's request she watched the latter from a window at York House, in view of St. James Palace. As the trumpeters sounded the heralds, cannons boomed, and flags were unfurled, she felt a hand grasp hers. He had snuck out to be with her to watch his own accession.

Wallis contentedly settled into life as the king's mistress. As he had all along, he continued to furnish her with expensive gifts of jewelry, furs, and an identical car to his, and he gave her a home to live in—he was to reside in Buckingham Palace. Edward, however, was not content. He wanted Wallis to be his bride, to which both she and Edward's mother objected; she on the grounds that she did not want to be queen. Nonetheless, she sought a divorce from Ernest, and it was granted. In celebration, Edward presented her with an engagement ring: the famed Mogul Emerald. Once belonging to the ancient rulers of India, the fabled stone had disappeared from public sight. The king had Cartier search for it; upon being located in Baghdad, it was purchased at a substantial premium and beautifully set for the king's presentation to Wallis.

On November 13, 1936, Edward was summoned to Buckingham Palace. He was informed that the government, including the prime minister, was against the marriage, and that they might resign if the king went through with it. Still the king stuck his ground. He told his beloved that he would either have to step down or they would be apart forever. Wallis prepared to leave London.

The king went to work on his abdication broadcast, aided by Winston Churchill, who had become supportive of the plan when he saw he could not sway Edward. On December 3, Wallis and the king clasped each other in a farewell embrace, she continuing to beg him not to go through with it. He told her,

> I don't know how it's all going to end. It will be some time before we can be together again. You must wait for me no matter how long it takes—I shall never give you up.

One week later, Edward made his abdication address over the radio to the people of England. He told them the decision to step down was his alone and that Wallis had begged him not to abdicate. Then he promised he would be of service to his country in any way possible in the future.

In the following years, after Edward and Wallis married, the world came to understand how devoted the couple was to each other. Their infamy turned to infinite popularity. After settling in France, although private citizens, they continued to be treated as royalty by virtually all except the British royal family—although they had the lifelong support of Churchill. In spite of the censure of his family, the duke and duchess of Windsor were as sought after as before and rose to the occasion. Wallis became renowned as a hostess and paragon of style. Over the years she amassed an amazing collection of jewels, all gifts from Edward. The duke pursued his passions for gardening and decorating their two homes, where they threw exquisite dinner parties. They were together for thirty-five years, until the end of the duke's life in 1972.

The duchess died fourteen years later in Paris. As she had requested, her jewels were auctioned by Sotheby's to benefit AIDS research, bringing in fifty million dollars. The bidding was frenzied as such celebrities as Elizabeth Taylor and Calvin Klein warred over the duke's tokens of his devotion to Wallis. Prince Charles also tried to win some Cartier panthers for his wife, Princess Diana. Unlike the duke, the current heir to the throne felt the price of love was too dear.

The Write Stuff

You would never guess from reading the novels of Susan Isaacs that she has been happily married for twenty-eight years to the same man. Or that this same husband, the well-known attorney Elkan Abramowitz, is not a lying, cheating lug as are some of the husbands she has written about in her bestsellers. In fact, Susan's husband is a truly romantic man.

Susan and Elkan met when she was twenty-three and working as an editorial assistant at *Seventeen* magazine. They were set up on a blind date by a distant cousin of Susan's who was married to Elkan's uncle. When the cousin told Susan Elkan's name, she politely declined. "Susan," said her mother, "you're not getting any younger."

Elkan was an assistant U.S. Attorney. For their first date, after speaking once on the phone, he took Susan to a New York Mets Old-Timers game. Die-hard Brooklyn Dodger fans, they both got teary when Roy Campanella was wheeled out onto the field. Then Elkan took her out for dinner and Susan thought to herself, "Wow, this is quite a guy." Elkan decided he wanted to marry her by the second date; Susan took a little longer to come around.

"I ought to have known, but my mother thought he was so marvelous that I decided there had to be something profoundly wrong with him," she said.

Years later, the couple was about to celebrate their twenty-fifth wedding anniversary; it was around the time Susan was on tour promoting her sixth novel, appropriately titled *After All These Years*. She got a call from her editor, who told her that he hated to do it to her, but he wanted to add one more city to the tour. Susan would be addressing the American Library Association in New Orleans the week of their wedding anniversary.

"Elkan can go with you," her editor said conciliatorily. Elkan, when asked, assured her that he didn't mind. The publishing house sent Susan two tickets to New Orleans. Her editor, who told her he would also be going, promised to take them out to dinner at a fancy restaurant and reminded Susan to pack something nice.

On the morning of the trip, just as they reached the airport, Elkan turned to Susan and said, "I don't want to go to New Orleans."

"I don't want to either, but we have to," she told him. "I promised." Elkan pulled out two airplane tickets and handed them to Susan.

"I want to go here," he said. As the taxi pulled up to the Air France terminal, Susan looked at the tickets. The destination read Charles de Gaulle Airport.

"Happy anniversary," Elkan said. He then told her how he had plotted, getting her editor to fake a trip to New Orleans to cover up for the real silver-anniversary plans.

Susan leaned close to Elkan as the Concorde lifted off to take them to Paris. When they arrived, they were whisked to the Ritz Hotel. Elkan had booked them for a week's stay, which included dinner each night in one of the city's finest restaurants and a day drive to Giverny.

Sometimes art doesn't imitate life at all.

The Bequest

A graduate of Bryn Mawr College is sent off into the world with a superb education and the notion that she can achieve anything. Such was the approach Joan Coward had to life after graduating from the women's college in 1945. In an era when most women hoped for a husband with a good career, Coward was determined to have her own professional success in business. By 1960, she was living in and working in Washington, D.C., as an economic analyst for the Civil Aeronautics Board; by the time she retired, she was the highest ranking woman there.

It was in 1960 that she met Harvey Wexler, who worked at the Air Transport Association of America. Wexler fell in love with the fiercely independent woman who modeled herself after Katharine Hepburn, also a Bryn Mawr graduate. Like her idol, the slim and beautiful Coward was brought up in a well-to-do New England family. She had refined taste and dressed impeccably.

Wexler, who went on to become a vice president at Continental Airlines, was an exceptionally bright man who had put himself through New York University in just two years, then got a business degree from Harvard. Like Coward, he was an intellectual whose interest lay in the field of economics. The event that had made the single most profound impact on him was as a child during the Depression—he had watched customers make a run on his father's bank, demanding their money. Although the government had ordered banks not to permit withdrawals, Wexler's father defied the order and gave back money to whoever asked for it. As a result, the next day customers were lining up to deposit money in Wexler's father's bank.

Although Wexler was deeply in love with Coward, she had decided she was "not the marrying kind." Their solution was for Coward to move into the same building as Wexler, where they each had one-bedroom apartments on different floors. For thirty years, the couple saw each other every day, escorting each other to functions and even traveling on vacation together. So reserved and private were they that not even their closest friends fully understood the true passion that existed between them.

When, in 1990, Coward died of cancer at the age of sixty-seven, Wexler was heartbroken. He searched for a way to memorialize her and called Bryn Mawr to see if he could donate money to the school in her name. Over the next few years, Wexler established a rapport with an economics professor at the college as well as the school's president. His connection to the place that had so shaped Coward's life seemed to ease his grief. Soon he saw what Coward had experienced at the school and was deeply impressed.

In the following years he had many phone conversations with the professor. Their discussions always centered on the many aspects of economics and never on Wexler's relationship with Coward. Perhaps through their talks, Wexler was able to re-create some of his finer moments with his companion. Wexler spoke about increasing the size of the gift and perhaps establishing a scholarship.

Then, in 1995, Wexler himself was diagnosed with cancer. Some of his friends were concerned that he might not have enough money to pay his medical bills, but he assured them he would be all right. In June 1996, the modest-living man's estate was settled. He had left his entire eleven-million-dollar fortune to Bryn Mawr, endowing a chair in economic history and another in political economy named after Coward. It was the single largest gift in the history of the college that had made him the happiest man in the world.

Abelard and Heloise

The story of Abelard and Heloise is one of the most beautiful and saddest love stories ever. To fully understand all that occurs within it, one must comprehend that in twelfth-century France, the religious life was considered the most important path a person could walk. Nonetheless, the fate of these lovers was enough to make any person question his or her faith.

Heloise was an orphan who until the age of fourteen lived in the convent of St. Marie of Argenteuil. Her sole relative was her uncle, Fulbert, who was a canon of Notre Dame, and who considered the prospect of raising his niece as impossible. Heloise thrived in the convent, reading voraciously, becoming fluent in five languages, including Greek and Latin, reading all the philosophers, and of course being superbly educated in theology. News of the amazing intellect of the teenage Heloise made its way to her uncle, who, eager to show her off, invited his niece to visit for two weeks.

The nuns reluctantly let their prize student go to Paris. Heloise had never set foot outside Argenteuil. Dressed in the gray convent uniform, her long brown hair pulled back, she looked with wonder at the streets of Paris, and, upon arriving at her uncle's, she immersed herself in his library. Each day her uncle returned home to share dinner with her and to discuss her new favorite book, Virgil's *Aeneid*. In fact, he so enjoyed her company that when two weeks passed no discussion was made of her return to the convent.

Heloise soon ventured out to hear lectures by the celebrated theologians of the time. The foremost teacher was Abelard, who often taught outdoors in the shadow of the cathedral. Abelard was famous for his many talents—not only a brilliant scholar and debater, he was also a poet, singer, and lute player. A first-born son, Abelard had given up his inheritance to become a clergyman. As he did in all things, he gave himself totally to his work, and even though he was permitted to marry, the exceptionally handsome young Abelard had chosen never to involve himself with women. Still, he was made of flesh and blood, and when the beautiful seventeen-year-old Heloise sat rapt as he lectured, he was smitten.

Abelard had heard of Heloise's brilliance and arranged a meeting with her by inviting himself to Fulbert's for dinner. At the close of the meal, Abelard made a suggestion: He asked to rent the spare room upstairs and offered to tutor Heloise, who was no longer receiving a formal education. Fulbert took up the suggestion, not only because Abelard was the foremost scholar of his time, but also because the canon knew he would be the envy of all his colleagues to have Abelard under his roof.

The love affair began immediately. Heloise believed

their relationship was the most natural thing on earth, for it was based entirely on love. Abelard, who was nearly twenty years older, knew the danger in what they were doing, but could not help himself. Soon he was writing poems and singing ballads about Heloise, and there was hardly a student of his who did not know of whom he sang. Heloise became pregnant and Abelard sent her home to his family to give birth to their son. Fulbert found out about the affair and threw Abelard out of his house. He demanded that Abelard marry Heloise and legitimize their relationship. Abelard agreed, but Heloise resisted. She didn't want to jeopardize Abelard's career: As a scholar, he would be less likely to receive teaching jobs if his employers knew they had to support his family as well. Marriage for Heloise was unnecessary—she was confident of their love and more than anything wanted Abelard to continue in his work.

Fulbert was not persuaded by Heloise's argument and presumably forced the wedding to save face for himself. Abelard and Heloise agreed to be wed as long as Fulbert told no one, which he promised. Feeling he had been deceived, however, he failed to keep his word. Soon everyone knew that Abelard and Heloise were husband and wife. His career now in jeopardy, Abelard asked Heloise to return to the convent at Argenteuil until he could resolve matters in Paris. Abelard visited Heloise once to reassure her. Together again, they could not resist their passion and made love on the stone floor of the refectory.

In Paris, Fulbert's rage simmered to the boiling point. He viewed Abelard's actions as self-serving and spiteful. His need for revenge could be contained no longer. One night, while the scholar slept, Fulbert and some cohorts broke into Abelard's dwelling. They took hold of him, and a doctor among Fulbert's men castrated him. At that moment Fulbert succeeded in ending what had undoubtedly been the truest love two people could share. For Abelard, it was not the pain of his physical wound that hurt so much, but the pity he received from everyone around him. It was more than he could take.

His solution was to become a monk and devote the rest of his life to the service of God. For Heloise, her life as she had anticipated it was over. She remained at the convent, and at Abelard's urging, took her vows. While by all appearances she was a perfect nun who eventually became Argenteuil's abbess, inside she questioned God and the fate delivered to her. For Heloise, only Abelard captured her soul.

Many years later, Heloise set up a new convent in a monastery Abelard had built at a time of seclusion and then later had been forced to abandon. Abelard lived nearby and helped the nuns restore Paraclete to working order and served as its spiritual master. Although it had been over a decade, Heloise was hopeful that their proximity would renew the love she had never ceased to let go of. When it seemed it was not to be, she wrote to Abelard a letter in which she poured out her heart and eloquently begged for a reunion with him: "My Abelard, it is you alone who can help me now. By you I was wounded and by you I must be healed. It is in your power, alone, to give me pain, to give me joy, to give me comfort."

Heloise was to remain disappointed in her husband, for his reply to her was to continue to give herself to God. Abelard had become a true monk, and her cries for him resulted only in words of comfort through religion. In fact, Abelard asked still more of her: that in the event of his death he wished to be buried at the Paraclete and that she must make sure of this. When death came for him, the all-forgiving Heloise had his body buried in front of the altar. Twenty years later, they finally shared the same space once more.

Love On-line

Internet dating has become the new wave of romance, but it has some serious drawbacks. This is especially true when the person you fall in love with turns out to live thousands of miles away, which is what happened to fifteen-year-old James W. of East Dundee, Illinois. One evening, while hanging out in *The X-Files* chat room, a comment on the screen caught his eye. The writer, also fifteen, mentioned that she spoke four languages, which interested James. He asked her a question about her linguistic skills and from there he and Alexandra Z. were burning up the modem lines.

The two began communicating constantly; when not on-line, by telephone and letter. They found they shared the same taste in music (Smashing Pumpkins and Pearl Jam) and movies *(Braveheart)*, as well as television shows (*The X-Files*, of course). James liked Alexandra because she was cool, got pretty good grades, had a good sense of humor; basically, "all the parts put together."

After a few months, James started itching to meet Alexandra face-to-face, but just didn't see how it was going to be possible. Alexandra lived in Hingham, Massachusetts. He decided he would tell her that he was going to be in the Boston area with his family for spring vacation and that he would come see her during that time. Then he left a note for his parents telling them not to worry, that he was going to be gone for a few days, but that he would be back. Having saved nearly $250 from his paper route and mowing lawns, James got on his bike with the intention of cycling to Hingham.

After a six-hour ride to Chicago, he realized the futility of his plan and took a Greyhound bus first to New York and then another one to Boston. From there he walked the twenty miles to Hingham, arriving on Alexandra's street at three-thirty in the morning, just over forty-eight hours after he had left East Dundee. With her house in sight, he was looking for someplace to sleep until morning when a cruising patrol car spotted him. The officers picked up James for being out after curfew. A phone call from the Hingham station house to the one in East Dundee revealed that they had a missing person on their hands. Despite James's pleas, he was put on the next flight back to Chicago. Not even a phone call was permitted. Alexandra never knew how close they had come to meeting in person.

Naturally James's parents were furious. They had learned of his plan from one of his friends. Under intense interrogation, the friend had confessed all, but he didn't know Alexandra's last name, having only the phone number of a friend of hers with whom he had been communicating on-line. A phone call to Alexandra's friend revealed that she knew nothing about James's plan.

As fate would have it, a reporter caught wind of James's amazing trip. After a story appeared in a local newspaper, some radio and television stations picked up on it. The good news is that James will be returning to Hingham on an all-expense-paid trip courtesy of the media.

How does Alexandra, now recovered from her initial shock, feel about finally getting to meet James? "She's pretty excited," James says. And what does James think will happen? "I just hope that it kind of works out, you know."

Lilies and Pickles

One of Russia's most famous singers is the opera sensation Galina Vishnevskaya. In the spring of 1955, already a star, Galina was introduced to another young star, the cellist Mstislav Rostropovich, at a reception. Although they were sitting at the same table, Galina paid him no further attention until she saw an apple rolling across the table in her direction, a sly allusion to the part of Paris in the opera *La Belle Hélène*. As Galina got up to go home, Rostropovich jumped up and asked to see her home.

The twenty-seven-year-old singer had been married for ten years to an older man for whom she cared deeply but from whom she had grown quite far apart as her career took off. As she walked with the cellist to her building, he began to flatter her, a scenario she was quite used to and which had little effect on her. As he said good night, he pulled a box of chocolates out of his coat and handed them to her. When she tried to refuse, he insisted she take them.

A year passed before she saw him again, at the

Prague Spring Festival, where she was to perform. On the first day, she joined all the other Soviet artists for breakfast at a restaurant. As she entered she saw Rostropovich, who headed right for her and escorted her to a chair next to him. She looked at him more closely, finding him to have a pleasant face and an elegant look. He asked her to call him Slava because his name was so difficult to pronounce, and asked if he might call her Galya, a familiar nickname for Galina. A little taken aback at his boldness, she hesitantly agreed. After lunch they walked out into the street, where Slava spotted a woman selling lilies of the valley. He bought the entire basketful and handed them to Galina.

For as long as she could remember, Galina had never felt like such a young girl. Every time she turned around, Slava was at her side. One evening in her dressing room, he fell to the floor just to kiss her feet because he found her legs so beautiful. As silly as his behavior seemed, it struck a long unplayed chord inside Galina. Another time, while taking a walk, they were unable to cross the street because of the huge puddles everywhere. When Galina asked what they should do, as it was late and they were expected for dinner, Slava took off his coat and laid it on the puddle for her to cross on. As they returned to the hotel, they passed a pickle shop that Galina was dismayed to see was closed. That evening after her performance, she opened the closet in her hotel room and jumped back in fear. Inside was a huge vase filled with lilies and pickles!

In her heart, Galina knew she was in love and that Slava was more of a husband to her in a few short days than was her own. After an official state visit to Yugoslavia, Galina went home to Moscow and told her husband that she was in love and that their marriage was over.

Although their previous decade had been marked by civility, her husband was beside himself and threatened suicide. Slava came by the apartment to pick her up, but with her husband in such a state, Galina felt she could not leave then. They agreed that the following day Galina would pretend to go to the theater and instead they would meet at noon at the Moscow Hotel.

As Galina prepared to leave the apartment the next morning, her husband asked her where she was going. When she told him the theater, he said he would walk her there. After he had dropped her off, she went in the entrance, ran across the stage, and exited out the back, running to get to the hotel. When she arrived, Slava was not there. On the street, she saw a taxi with a swarm of people around it. As Galina got closer she saw they were staring because the cab was totally filled with flowers. In the middle of all the lilies sat Slava.

This was not the type of thing one saw on a Moscow street, and the crowd looked at her to see what would happen next. Even the cab driver was silent—he was convinced that this moment would be a turning point in the young man's life. Galina got in.

The Groom Came C.O.D.

Sometimes you have to hit a man over the head to get his attention or, in the case of Carmen C., threaten to steal his truck. A single mother living in New York City's Washington Heights, Carmen developed a huge crush on her

UPS delivery man, Louis M. For three years, whenever she saw him in the building, Carmen would try and engage him in conversation. But Louis was always busy with his deliveries and seemed oblivious to her efforts.

Carmen turned to her nine-year-old son Dwayne for advice.

"Mommy, order things through the mail—he *has* to come to the house," Dwayne suggested. "Then you offer him something to drink and ask him in."

"Out of the mouths of babes," thought Carmen, as she rifled through catalogs. Soon she was ordering merchandise by the truckload. Nearly every week Louis would come to the apartment to drop off Carmen's newest order. Each time she would offer him something to drink. This seemed to confuse Louis, who always politely turned her down, professing he had to get back to work. After a while Carmen had nothing to show for her efforts except a huge stack of bills and a pile of stuff she hadn't really needed anyhow. She stopped ordering from catalogs, explaining, "This man was too expensive for me!"

Some months later, Carmen saw Louis's truck parked outside the building. Before she realized what she was doing, she ran out to the street where it was parked.

"I'm going to steal your truck," she shouted to Louis when he appeared.

He looked at Carmen as if seeing her for the first time. Gently he placed his hand over hers.

"You can have it," he said.

"No, thank you," she answered. "I'd much rather have the driver."

Now when Louis takes a package to Carmen's building, he's bringing it home.

Nicholas and Alexandra

Nicholas, the last tsar of Russia, first laid eyes on his future wife, Alexandra, in 1884, when she was twelve and he was sixteen. Nicky was heir to the Russian throne and Alix was a German princess who had been raised in England by her maternal grandmother, Queen Victoria. The young couple met at the wedding festivities of her sister Ella to Nicholas's uncle, a grand duke and the brother of the tsar.

Nicholas fell instantly in love with the pale, blond beauty. To win her affections, he asked his mother for a diamond brooch to give her. During a quiet moment at Peterhof, the imperial dacha, Nicky bestowed the gift on Alix, who accepted it, but immediately had misgivings. Fearing she had acted improperly, she returned the brooch to Nicholas while dancing with him at a ball the next day, thrusting the beautiful present into his hand and accidentally stabbing him with it.

Nicholas was beside himself with distress but agreed to his father's demand that, for political reasons, he not seek an engagement with Alix. Nicholas, while daring not to disobey his father, formulated a plan: He refused to marry a French princess or any other girl his family brought before him.

Five years later, Alix returned to Russia to visit her sister, but also to be "inspected" by the royal family, who had begun to see that the heir was unbudging. Again, they rejected her. The official reason given was that she would not convert to Orthodoxy. Since Alix was deeply religious, she went along with their statement.

When she returned for another visit a year later, Nicholas was forbidden to see her. He wrote in his diary, "My dream is one day to marry Alix H. Have loved her for a long time, but even more deeply and strongly since 1889, when she spent six weeks of the winter in Petersburg. Have fought my feeling for a long time, trying to deceive myself with the impossibility of my cherished dream coming true . . ."

Nicholas silently played a waiting game, never indicating a desire to marry anyone else nor mentioning Alix. Instead he staged a quiet rebellion, and spent his time in preparation for his future position as tsar, traveling abroad a great deal. Finally, in April 1894, the couple was to meet again at another wedding, that of Alix's brother, Ernie, to a German princess. Nicholas's family realized it was inevitable that he would see Alix and that he still wanted to marry her, so they devised to announce the engagement at the wedding. Nicholas formally proposed and Alix tearfully accepted. Ten years after first giving it to her, Nicky gave Alix the diamond brooch again, along with a ruby ring.

The married life of Nicholas and Alexandra was an extraordinary one. Nicholas's father died several months after their engagement, and so the couple married in the weeks after the tsar's death, a rushed wedding sadly tainted with funereal tones. In the next ten years the couple had four daughters and then finally a son. Their children were of paramount importance to them; as devoted as Nicky and Alix were to each other, they were to their offspring. Nicky loved to bestow jewels on his wife, which she in turn bestowed on their daughters.

Though they were often apart due to the tsar's duties, Nicholas and Alexandra managed to spend every anniversary together, and she always wore the brooch he had first given her at Peterhof. They wrote constant love letters to each other when he was away. On the twenty-first anniversary of their engagement, they were apart for the first time. Alix wrote to him to let him know she was wearing her brooch and how happy she was with him.

Their idyllic existence was not to last. Russia was a country in flux, and in 1917 the Communist revolution began. Nicholas was overthrown by the Bolsheviks and was sent with his family into exile in Siberia. On July 16, 1918, he and his family were taken to the cellar of their house and shot.

In a bizarre twist, when their assassins began firing on the family, many of the bullets bounced off them: Alix and her daughters had sewn their jewels into their corsets for safekeeping. Alix's diamond brooch was pinned close to her heart.

"I Love You, Alice B. Toklas"

Gertrude Stein and Alice B. Toklas were the most famous American couple in Paris in the 1920s. Stein hosted a weekly salon in their home where writers, artists, and other members of the intellectual elite gathered. Some of the regulars at the Salon d'Automne were Picasso, Matisse, Renoir, Gauguin, Cézanne, Sherwood Anderson, Hemingway, and Fitzgerald. In exchange for advice and absinthe from Gertrude, who was a second mother to her brood of young men, her charges gave back to her their art and appreciation.

Gertrude and Alice met on Alice's first day in the City of Lights through a mutual friend. The thirty-year-old Alice had come to Paris to escape the stifling Victorian sensibility of her life in San Francisco, where she had been unhappily looking after her father, brother, and uncles since she was twelve. A lover of literature and music and a secret lesbian, Alice knew she would never find happiness there, but she had hardly imagined how happy she would become in Paris.

Gertrude invited Alice to come for a walk with her the day after they met. The next morning, Alice's traveling companion Harriet wanted to go to lunch in the Bois de Boulogne, so Alice sent a note to Gertrude saying that she would be late. When she finally arrived at Gertrude's apartment, a half hour late, Gertrude was furious and completely enraged. No one had ever done this to her before, she ranted. But she decided they should go anyway, and the couple spent the afternoon walking, finally stopping at a pastry shop, something they would habitually do together for the rest of their lives. The afternoon ended with Gertrude issuing another invitation to Alice, this time for dinner.

The relationship remained one of ever deepening friendship, with Gertrude and Alice seeing each other constantly, until the following summer, when they went together to Italy. It was there, on a hilltop among the ancient ruins and idyllic scenery of Fiesole, that their relationship was defined. One afternoon, they found themselves in a beautiful garden and Gertrude summoned up her courage. On the Italian hilltop she proposed to Alice, saying, "Care for me. I care for you in every possible way." Gertrude was asking Alice to become her wife, in essence.

A weeping Alice replied, "I am your bride."

The two settled into life together, with Alice supplying Gertrude with everything she needed, mainly love and support. She also looked after the apartment, cooked the meals, typed the pages that Gertrude had written the night before, and served as Gertrude's sounding board. During the Saturday salons, Alice would sit with the wives discussing such trivial things as perfume and recipes, while Gertrude held court with the men. Although Alice was a discreet, almost ghostlike presence—she was rail thin, in sharp contrast to Gertrude's two hundred pounds—she missed nothing and provided Gertrude with an analysis of her likes and dislikes at the close of the weekly salon. Hardly any of the visitors, such as Ezra Pound or T. S. Eliot, understood the power Alice wielded: Their invitation to return was subject to Alice's approval; without it, Gertrude's role as a cultivator of young talent was moot. When the beloved and depressed F. Scott Fitzgerald came to her once claiming a lack of inspiration, Gertrude sent him home to write the best thing he could. When he produced the completed *Tender Is the Night*, he proffered it to her and asked if this is what she had meant, and she answered in the affirmative.

As Gertrude was to these young men, so Alice was to Gertrude. When Gertrude was unsuccessful in finding a publisher for one of her books, Alice created Plain Edition, and published and promoted the volume. Alice was also able to sift through Gertrude's famously dense and esoteric writing and get right to the heart of it. It was she who spotted the famous line, "A rose is a rose is a rose."

Still, life was hard. Broke and desperate, Gertrude sat down one day determined to create a commercial success. The work that ensued was *The Autobiography of Alice B. Toklas*, in which Gertrude told Alice's life story as though she were Alice. It was a sensation, becoming a hit with the public and critics alike. The book that made Gertrude Stein a legend was also a supreme act of love.

The two lived out their lives in Paris and other places in France during World War II, during which they drove a broken-down Ford truck around France bringing supplies to their "boys" in the army. Stein died of cancer in 1946, leaving Alice without a raison d'être. When Yale University agreed to be home to the Stein archives, Alice threw herself into the compilation of the project, as well as the publication of some of Stein's unpublished writing. Later Alice herself published a book—a cookbook of recipes of meals she made for them, spiced with anecdotes of their life together. To no one's surprise, the recipes are very rich.

A Bed of Roses

It was Elizabeth H.'s infectious smile that caused Keith S. to fall for her the moment he saw her. Petite, vivacious, and raven-haired, Elizabeth was producing a fashion show in New York City to which a mutual friend had brought

Keith. Naturally, Elizabeth was crazed with taking care of all the show's details, and was a little annoyed by this good-looking, strawberry-blond man with fabulous eyes who had attached himself to her side.

Keith was patient, and by the end of the evening he had gotten Elizabeth to unwind and go dancing with him. Eight months later, they were living together. Elizabeth's friends always told her how lucky she was because Keith was such a romantic.

Elizabeth's thirtieth birthday was several months after they met, and Keith wanted to make it extraordinarily special. While Elizabeth was at work, Keith set to decorating her apartment. Taking the petals from eight dozen roses, he completely covered her bed with them, leaving uncovered only the outline of his body. In the middle of that he lay a single long-stemmed red rose. When Elizabeth got home, he opened a bottle of Cristal and then took her to a wonderful French restaurant for dinner. She was even more surprised the next evening, when they arrived at a restaurant where twenty friends were waiting to join them for dinner.

On the first anniversary of their meeting, after being out late the night before, Keith woke a protesting Elizabeth up at six in the morning. He handed her a packed bag, and before she knew it they were in a limousine heading for the airport. Soon they were traveling first-class to Los Angeles, near Keith's hometown. When they arrived, they drove to a marina and boarded Keith's waiting thirty-foot sailboat for a three-day cruise to Catalina.

After these romantic surprises, Elizabeth's friends began to kid her that he would have a hard time outdoing himself. So for her thirty-first birthday, Keith told her in advance that he would be taking her away for a few days.

The night before the trip, he handed her a brochure for an old inn in Washington, Connecticut, which was ranked as one of the best in the country. He also showed her four wrapped presents but told her she couldn't open them until the following day.

After spending her birthday outdoors, playing tennis and relaxing, they went back to their room to get ready for dinner. As they sat on the balcony taking in the magnificent view, Keith handed Elizabeth her gifts. In the first box was a guide book to Costa Rica, where they were planning a trip. In the second box was a sweater Elizabeth had wanted. The third was in a shoe box. After unwrapping one layer, Elizabeth realized there was a second. After she unwrapped the second, she saw a little black box. As she opened the little box to see a beautiful diamond ring, she heard Keith's voice:

"Will you marry me?"

After Elizabeth said yes, she opened the fourth box, which contained a bottle of Dom Pérignon. Toasting the future, they drank it together.

The Taj Mahal

No greater monument to love has ever been built than India's Taj Mahal. Described as "rising above the banks of the river like a solitary tear suspended on the cheek of time," by the poet Debendranath Tagore, the magnificent structure was created as a mausoleum for the second wife of the Emperor Shah Jahan; she died while giving birth to their fourteenth child in 1631. The emperor was so over-come with grief at his wife's death that he ordered the Taj Mahal built in the imperial city of Agra, on the bank of the Yamuna River. Made of pure white marble and inlaid with over forty types of semiprecious stones, there is no other structure in the world that comes close to it in the intensity of detail and craftsmanship.

It is said that when Mumtaz Mahal—whose name means the Chosen One of the Palace, conferred upon her by the emperor on the day of their marriage—died, Shah Jahan's beard turned from black to white overnight. According to legend, his grief was so deep that he did not appear in public for a week following her death, and for two years gave up feasting, music, entertainment, even sex.

Instead the emperor threw himself into preserving his wife's memory by creating a symbol of a love that was stronger than death. What he proposed for the Taj Mahal was so extensive that it took twenty thousand men working for twenty-two years to complete, according to one estimate. Of the forty varieties of semiprecious stones chosen for the building were carnelian, agate, amethyst, jasper, green beryl, chalcedony, onyx, and coral. Set in milk white marble, the stones were carved into the shapes of flowers such as lily, narcissus, iris, and tulip, which were chosen because in Islam flowers were symbols of the kingdom of God. Upon viewing the mausoleum in 1926, the writer Aldous Huxley said, "The smallest rose or poppy on the royal tombs is an affair of twenty or thirty carnelians, onyxes, agates, chrysolites."

The structure of the Taj Mahal is not only unique in its absolute symmetry, but created in accordance with what is written in the Koran. The building and grounds are intended to represent the paradise of life after death. Leading up to the building are four canals, which symbolize the Gardens of Paradise in the Koran, and the location of the building at the northern point of the gardens (and not in the center) reinforces that notion. The use of many gentle curves and marble that is white (and thereby chaste) was intended to highlight the effeminate nature of the architecture and remind visitors of the emperor's beloved wife.

Black marble was used to inlay the white walls with inscriptions from the Koran. Written in calligraphy—considered the pinnacle of artistic expression of the time—over the main gate to the Taj Mahal is an inscription that invites Mumtaz Mahal to peacefully return to her Lord in this paradise created for her. There is a mosque located to the west of the building for the faithful to pray for the dead, and a guest house located on the east side, both in red sandstone, maintaining the absolute perfect symmetry of the architecture.

The only nonsymmetrical aspect of the Taj Mahal is the placement of the tombs, and the reason is ironic. It is believed that the mausoleum was created solely for Mumtaz Mahal, and so her beautifully carved marble crypt was placed directly in the center of the building facing Mecca. The notion that she alone was intended to rest there is supported by Shah Jahan's plan to create a mausoleum in black marble for himself on the other side of the Yamuna River. As fate would have it, the emperor was overthrown and jailed by his son Aurangzeb in 1658. He spent the last eight years of his life imprisoned in the Red Fort—situated just above the bend in the river where the Taj Mahal sat—looking out a small window at the glorious monument to Mumtaz Mahal. After the emperor's death, his son had him buried next to his wife in the Taj Mahal, thus causing the sole disturbance to its perfect symmetry.

"You Know How to Whistle, Don't You?"

Humphrey Bogart was already famous in Hollywood as the star of such films as *Casablanca* and *The Maltese Falcon* when an unknown young actress named Lauren Bacall was cast opposite him in *To Have and Have Not*. Bacall was under the tutelage of the director Howard Hawks, whose wife Slim had spotted Bacall modeling in *Harper's Bazaar*. For months Hawks had guided Bacall through acting classes, and the deepening of her voice to its famous husky tone, until he felt she was ready for a job. What he didn't tell her was that her first role was to be a starring one.

Bogie and Bacall's first reactions to each other were less than auspicious. When Bacall was told Bogie would be in the film, she thought, "How awful to be in a picture with that mug, that illiterate. He mustn't have a brain in his head. He won't be able to think or talk about anything." Bogie recalled taking a look at the willowy eighteen-year-old he would soon be madly in love with and thinking, "She's a very long girl." At five-eight and a half, she was a half inch shorter than he, but with heels, she towered over him.

Hawks had promised Bogie before he met Betty, as she was known, that his costar would be as insolent as he was. Bogie was skeptical.

The first scene Bogart and Bacall filmed together was the one for which they would always be known. Bacall, wearing a robe, comes into Bogart's hotel room carrying an unlit cigarette. After Bogie lights it for her, she says thanks and leaves the room. She returns to utter her famous line, in which she tells him that if he needs her, he should whistle: "You know how to whistle, don't you? You just put your lips together and blow." Her head was tilted down and her eyes were gazing up, and in that moment she created her movie stardom, as well as what would become known as "the Look."

While it seemed to many that theirs was a typical onset romance, common in the making of movies, friends of Bogie soon realized that he was serious about her. Although Bogie was married to his third wife, Mayo, a former actress, the marriage was over in every way except legally. A heavy drinker, Mayo was fiercely jealous and prone to physical fights with her husband. Bogie was desperately guilty about wanting to end the marriage—as well as terrified that Mayo would commit suicide—but would not give up Bacall.

Bacall coolly sat back and let the inevitable play itself out. While this took a good deal longer than she expected, with Bogie going back to Mayo twice out of guilt, in the end she got her man. Bacall knew she would prevail if she was patient. Bogie was also concerned that a marriage to a girl Bacall's age—she was nineteen and he was forty-four—might not last. After confiding this concern to his *Casablanca* costar Peter Lorre, Lorre gave him the best advice a friend could give. "What's the difference? It's better to have five good years than none at all."

While Bogie agonized, the two began work on another of their famous film collaborations, *The Big Sleep*. By Christmas of 1944, Bogie had had enough of Mayo's mania, and she finally agreed to a divorce. Bacall was delighted and said, "I had everything I wanted. I had Bogie." For Christmas Bogie gave her a gold whistle inscribed, "If you want anything, just whistle."

On January 31, 1945, Bogie announced to the press that he was getting divorced and would marry Bacall. Only he had not asked her. They had agreed to meet in New York, and when she arrived at Grand Central Station, she was set upon by reporters. One asked if she would be marrying Bogie. "He'll have to ask me first," she quipped.

In May of that year, his divorce came through. Bogie never formally proposed to Bacall, instead asking her to meet him in Chicago, where he had to go for business. "Then we'll go on to Louis Bromfield's [a writer friend] farm and get married," he said. "Might as well kill two birds with one stone." Bacall didn't complain.

After they were married, Bacall and Bogie had a set routine that involved both of them going to the studio together in the morning. Since they hated to be apart for more than three hours at a time, when possible they met for lunch, and at the end of the day the one who was finished shooting first would wait for the other. They studied scripts at night and went to bed early. On weekends they went on Bogie's boat or Bacall stayed home while he went with his male friends. She was content to be a stay-at-home wife and Bogie was thrilled. Their marriage produced a son, Stephen, named after Bogie's character in *To Have and Have Not*, and a daughter, Leslie. A father for the first time at forty-nine, Bogie wasn't sure about how he felt about such domestication and responsibility, but it turned out that he loved it. Once a heavy drinker, Bogie had mellowed at last. Until his death in 1957 from cancer, the marriage was a deeply loving one that had lasted and survived all bets on the contrary.

"Light My Fire"

"It was the old story," Kiva said. "We met at work." Which seems ordinary enough, unless his job is swallowing swords and pounding nails into various openings in his head, and hers is fire-eating. They worked in Coney Island, Brooklyn, the Broadway of sideshows.

Fredini, who is known as the Human Blockhead, and Kiva had actually met once before, when Kiva came to Sideshows at the Seashore in Coney Island looking for someone to replace her in a fire-eating act. She had made the awful mistake of performing outdoors on a windy day, badly burning herself. Her face was wrapped in bandages the first time she saw Fred, whose impression of her was "What an idiot."

A Russian émigré, Kiva decided she wanted to become a sideshow performer the moment she heard such a thing actually existed. Two years after her inauspicious first visit to Sideshows, she was back in Coney Island. She had gotten a job as an apprentice fire-eater at a freak museum that was billing itself as sideshow, but that only had photographs of legendary freaks and one live act. Kiva was "really hankering for a job at the real sideshow," where Fredini was the star act.

Most nights, after their shows were over, the Coney Island performers would get together under the G Top, the historical name for the performer's tent, which in Coney Island is located on top of the freak museum. Fred, his good friend the Illustrated (tattooed) Man, and other freaks would hang out on the balcony unwinding, watching Kiva perform her act down below. Fred and Kiva started to become close friends and soon he joined the other performers who would go to Kiva's to play cards several times a week. As a seasoned veteran, Fred kept an eye out for Kiva, who had a tendency to be impressionable. She once nearly joined a traveling freak show whose boss had lured her with an offer of luxurious living quarters and good money. Fred, knowing it was a scam and that the show's performers became virtual slaves to their boss, talked Kiva out of it.

Finally Kiva's big break came. One afternoon, as she was taking tickets at the museum, Dick Zigin, who runs Sideshows by the Seashore, walked across the street. The contortionist hadn't shown up for work and Zigin told Kiva if she wanted the job she would have to go on in ten minutes. She quit the freak museum on the spot and ran to get in costume for her performance.

In Fred's words: "She was in the blade box, which is a cabinet that eighteen solid-steel blades go through. You have to twist and contort to get inside it. It's traditionally the job that's hardest to keep filled. They work the hardest and make the least amount of money. Someone always quits in the middle of the summer."

So Kiva was then a bona fide member of the world's most established sideshow. That winter the company was given a run in New York's SoHo area, and when the fire-eater's contract expired, Kiva was promoted. Since Kiva was also a costume designer, Zigin hired her to make the costumes for the winter season. It was about this time that Kiva realized, "I had a wicked crush on Fred." Sadly, he was oblivious. Despite many subtle hints and the help of the Illustrated Man, Fred was unaware of her feelings.

When it was Fred's turn to be fitted for his winter costume, Kiva realized it was time for action. Fred arrived at her apartment and Kiva went to work. She took two hours to measure him for his pants alone.

"All of a sudden I realized what was going on," Fred said. "It was the best fitting I ever had."

Fast-forward several years to May 1996. Fred and Kiva decided to make it legal and no one was more thrilled than Dick Zigin. For Zigin and Sideshows by the Seashore, it was the event of the decade. The week before the summer season began again at Coney Island, Zigin created his biggest performance ever: the Wedding of the Freaks!

All of Coney Island turned out for the nuptials. Naturally, the Illustrated Man was the best man. The ring bearer, wearing a tiny tuxedo, was the couple's two-year-old son Kostya, who had performed the summer before as the Psychic Baby. The wedding party included other performers, and the music was by Mr. Spoons, a one-man utensil band and New York fixture. Zigin was ecstatic.

In the summer of 1996 Kiva expanded her act to walking on glass. Under doctor's orders, she was forbidden to fire-eat; Fred and Kiva will be adding one more freak to the family.

"Speak for Yourself, John"

Among the Pilgrim settlers who came to America on the *Mayflower* in 1620 was thirty-six-year-old Myles Standish, the captain and military commander of the new settlement in New England.

Standish had married a woman named Rose shortly before leaving England, and she accompanied him to the New World. Sadly, she did not survive the exposure to new diseases and the freezing climate of the first winter. In fact, by the spring of the new year, fewer than half of the original settlers were still alive.

Standish decided shortly after the death of Rose that the best solution to his lonely state would be to remarry and start a family. Although very little time had passed since his wife's death, he sought the hand of Priscilla Mullins, the attractive young daughter of William Mullins.

A short, broad-shouldered, muscular man with a red beard already flecked with white, Standish was not much to look at. As was the custom, he sent a messenger named John Alden to Priscilla's father to ask his permission to request his daughter's hand in marriage. Mr. Mullins offered no objections but informed Alden that his daughter must be consulted.

Alden, who had a fair and ruddy complexion and an excellent physique, called upon Priscilla. After she had listened with respectful attention to his message, she paused, looking intently at him. Then Priscilla said, "Prithee, John, why do you not speak for yourself?"

For John Alden, it was a most happy day.

Myles Standish took the defeat in stride. He later married a woman named Barbara, with whom he had six sons and a daughter. A generation later, things came full circle, when his son Alexander married Sarah Alden, Priscilla and John's daughter.

The Unused Heart

Margot Fonteyn was one of this century's most brilliant ballerinas, whose career spanned decades. Onstage her partnership with Rudolf Nureyev was the stuff of legend. Offstage her partnership with her husband, Robert Arias, was a testament to true love.

The half-Brazilian Fonteyn grew up first in Shanghai and then moved to England, where she was able to develop as a dancer. By the age of nineteen she had danced the principal roles in *Giselle*, *Swan Lake*, and *The Sleeping Beauty* as a member of Sadler's Wells company in London. While immensely accomplished in her profession, Fonteyn had barely a chance to develop personally. Immensely shy, she was most comfortable when she was onstage, dancing and transformed into a character. It was there that she let her emotions and passion emerge.

Margot and Arias, who was known as Tito, first met at a party at Cambridge, where he was a student. He and his brother had done a rumba, and the eighteen-year-old Margot fell instantly in love with the black-haired, black-eyed boy with the coffee complexion. Tito came back the next day to see her and would often visit her in her dressing room as she put on her makeup, telling her stories of his native Panama. While it was clear he had a deep affection for her, Margot's feelings ran deeper. When he returned home for the summer and did not write to her, Margot was heartbroken. She did not see him again until the following May. He put his arms around her, holding her close, and asked her if she was still his. Her hardened heart spoke the word she did not mean: "No."

Over the next year he took her out to dinner several times, but Margot refused to let herself feel too much. Then the war came and Margot let him slip from her mind and focused on dancing. In the years that followed, she became famous. Still, at the age of twenty-nine, Margot realized that she had nothing besides her work. She was neither married nor had someone to love, and felt she had only six good years of dancing left.

In the fall of 1953, Margot was at the Met in New York dancing *The Sleeping Beauty*. A stagehand delivered a visiting card bearing Tito's name and a message saying that he would visit her backstage. He arrived after the first act and asked her to dinner, but she had already made plans; he said he would call the next day. Early the next morning her phone rang. Tito said he was leaving for Panama at noon; could they have breakfast? Margot protested, saying she wasn't awake yet, but Tito insisted. Minutes later, he was sitting cross-legged on her floor, just as he used to do backstage when Margot was making up, and talking with her. He asked her to marry him, although he had just told her he was married with three children.

She laughed, but he said he was serious and he would get divorced.

The next day he sent one hundred long-stemmed red roses. Shortly thereafter, he called from Panama to say his wife had agreed to a divorce. He flew back to New York and began wooing Margot madly. Ironically, she was now the ambivalent one and he the pursuer. He gave her beautiful jewelry and furs and took her anywhere she wanted. He was the Panamanian ambassador to the United Nations and was constantly flying home, and every time he returned to Margot he was thinner—he had previously grown very fat—and happier. In a twenty-three-page letter, he told her that he had never stopped thinking about her or loving her in the fourteen years they had been apart.

After so many lonely years, Fonteyn asked Tito to wait while she tried to find her "unused heart." She was examining feelings she had been out of touch with for so long. Finally, Fonteyn realized that she loved him and agreed to marry him.

Fonteyn settled slowly into the life of being the wife of an ambassador, as well as continuing her career. Though weathering Tito's political life was not always easy—at one point she was placed under arrest and deported from Panama while Tito took part in a failed revolution attempt—she remained his stalwart companion.

Over the next few years, Margot formed her famed partnership with the Russian dancer Rudolf Nureyev. At forty-three, Margot was dancing ballets with him that she had been dancing since 1938, the year Nureyev was born. Still, the chemistry between the two was undeniable and they danced to sell-out crowds everywhere. Any chance that she would retire was put aside.

Tito, meanwhile, was running for a position in the national assembly. An aide of his asked Tito to make him a substitute deputy, after the election; Tito assured him by message that he would do so if he received the proper number of votes. Enraged, the aide drove and intercepted Tito's car, shooting him five times. Tito was instantly paralyzed. Margot flew to his side and moved him to a famed rehabilitation institution in England. There he took a severe turn for the worse, slipped into a coma, and nearly died.

Though Tito slowly recovered, he remained a quadriplegic. Often he asked Margot to let him die, but she would not. Instead, she became his pillar of strength. Two and a half years after being shot, Tito made a bittersweet return to Panama to fill the job for which he had been elected in the national assembly. Still in demand, to her amazement, Margot continued to dance. She celebrated her forty-eighth birthday onstage, at New York's Lincoln Center, with the audience singing her "Happy Birthday" at the end of the evening.

October 1968 brought a coup to Panama, and Tito finally resigned himself to being out of politics in his homeland. In exile again, they returned when they could two years later. Tito was determined that he could be of some assistance to his people. Margot continued to work, for love. When once asked how they managed to stay together through such tragedy, Tito replied, "I think. She moves."

Love in the Twilight Years

You're never too old to fall in love. Ninety-year-old Mary K. found this out when she accepted a proposal of marriage from her eighty-seven-year-old boyfriend.

Men had always chased after Mary as a young woman, but she found they wanted to get serious so fast that she never got a chance to really know them. Finally, after a failed romance in college, she gave up on men and marriage. Mary was a high school Latin teacher for forty years, and then she and her sister moved to a retirement community in Lacey, Washington. Not one for sitting still, she became active in the running of the community, helping finance the building of a management center, and editing the community newspaper.

In 1973, Johan A. and his wife moved in next door. Mary, her sister, and Johan's wife were thick as thieves. The neighbors had Thanksgiving together every year. About twelve years after arriving, Johan's wife came down with severe senile dementia, often wandering away from home until Johan went and found her. The stress for Johan was unbearable, but he never complained. Finally, a concerned Mary called his son in California. He intervened, and Johan's wife was put into a home where she could be well taken care of, and she eventually passed away in 1991.

Naturally Johan was lonely. Like Mary, he didn't think much of sitting around. A retired civil engineer, he had been in charge of most of the New York City water-supply system and later was put in charge of the EPA lab at Annapolis. After his wife left, Mary says, "He was so lonely that he'd come over. He'd find some excuse. He'd just stay and talk and talk. We got a little better acquainted that way. I got to know him and trust him and that was why I was able to get so close to him." Then Mary's sister died of cancer, and Mary found herself on her own, with just Johan for close company.

One day she was over at Johan's house when his family was visiting ("Sometimes I'd take him something or go over for advice because he's a terribly smart man"), and she noticed that his grandsons were staring impolitely at her. Curious, she asked their mother about their behavior. She explained to Mary that they were doing so because "Grandfather looks so much younger and he looks so happy." Then Johan's son called him to find out if anything was going on between him and Mary, who got mad because she didn't feel it was any of their business.

"I said I didn't like that," Mary explains. "Right after that he boomed out, 'I like you!' That was the first time he ever said that he liked me. I was so surprised by that. Two years later he came over and asked me what medicine I took. He wanted to know what I was up against. All I could tell him was that I took an aspirin a day and I took some drops in one of my eyes. The next day he came over and proposed to me. And I was so surprised. I said yes because he just seemed like one of the family by then. I guess he kissed me then. He told me after that he wrote down in his calendar that that was their first kiss."

Several months later Mary and Johan exchanged their wedding vows among their family and friends in the center's building she had helped erect. As they looked out over the beautiful open fields around the former dairy farm that was now their home, they promised to love and cherish each other for the rest of their days.

Beatrice

There is perhaps no greater work of literature than *The Divine Comedy*, by the Italian poet Dante Alighieri. Considered a cornerstone of Western literature, it consists of the famed poet's imaginary travels through hell, purgatory, and finally heaven. Throughout his journeys, Dante meets many great men of ancient times. When he gets to heaven, his guide is a woman named Beatrice.

Dante first laid eyes on the actual Beatrice when his father took him to a party at the home of Beatrice's father in 1274. Dante was then just nine, Beatrice eight. The image of her that day, a quiet angel in a crimson dress, never left his memory and served to inspire him for the rest of his life. Both children were to have arranged marriages to others, so the notion of a relationship between the two was impossible.

Nonetheless, Dante was so inspired by Beatrice that he began to write sonnets about her. In one he writes, "It became my purpose to write down words which should make understood the wonderful and excellent effects she had." Dante's poems and sonnets were incredibly beautiful, such as this one:

My lady carries love within her eyes:
Hence all who look at her are lovely made.
He who doth pass her by must turn his head,
And him she speaks to, tremble in such wise
That his abashed face grows pale and wan,
And he doth sigh for every fault he has.
Anger and pride before her footsteps run.
Ah ladies, help me honor her and praise!
All sweetness, every modest thought there is,
Is born in his heart who her speaking hears.
Blessed is he who first did her behold.
And when she doth but smile, what she
    appears
Cannot be held in memory or told.
It is too rare and noble a miracle.

Beatrice was aware of Dante's love for her, and some suggest that he actually courted her, but they rarely met face-to-face. He was known to be a lady's man, and perhaps his reputation prevented further encounters. As well, Beatrice was from one of the wealthiest and most noble families in Florence, making contact with her difficult. It is known, however, that he saw her often from afar and used these moments as inspiration. One time, she greeted him as they passed in the street. Dante wrote of it, "As that was the first time that her words set forth to come to my ears, such sweetness possessed me that as one drunken I departed from all people and withdrew to the solitude of my room, and began thinking of this most courteous one."

In 1290, the twenty-four-year-old Beatrice died of the black plague and Dante was plunged into a deep depression. Unable to do anything but grieve, he could not write. When he did begin to work again, he wrote about her.

During Italy's civil war, Dante supported the losing side and was sent into exile in 1301. It was during this time that he wrote the majority of *The Divine Comedy*, dreaming of Beatrice as an angel in heaven, waiting to take him home.

Starting Over

In modern times, there was scarcely so controversial a couple as John Lennon and Yoko Ono. As in love and devoted to each other as they were, Beatles' fans everywhere reviled them, believing that Ono broke up the band. In fact, it was Lennon himself who broke up the Beatles by deciding it was time to move on. For him, this meant moving forward with someone who shared his vision of the future.

John Lennon, Paul McCartney, Ringo Starr, and George Harrison—the Beatles—were one of the most popular bands ever. The four young men from Liverpool went from broke unknowns to millionaires overnight when their second single, "Please, Please Me," went to number one in just seven weeks in 1963. They immediately released an album and were an instant phenomenon. One of the things that made the band so successful was that they wrote all the songs themselves—virtually unheard-of at the time—providing their audience with the freshest sound they had heard in years. The good looks and identical haircuts and suits of the foursome didn't hurt either.

Lennon had married his college sweetheart, Cynthia, when she discovered she was pregnant. They had a son, Julian, and were together for four years, but success and fame changed John. He was desperately in need of finding peace and solace within himself, and the mania for the Beatles denied him that.

One day in London in 1966, Lennon walked into a gallery where Ono was putting the finishing touches on an exhibit of her avant-garde art. She ignored the Beatle as he walked around in amazement at the work. One piece of art required him to climb a ladder to look at a black canvas that was hanging from the ceiling. A pair of binoculars hung on a hook nearby. Lennon looked through them and saw that on the canvas written in tiny letters was the word *yes*. He loved it.

He and Ono became good friends. She was Japanese-born, but had emigrated with her family to the United States, where she attended Sarah Lawrence College, studying art and music. She dropped out to marry a musician, then later divorced him and married a movie director with whom she had a child and moved to London.

As Lennon grew emotionally farther apart from Cynthia, he fell in love with Yoko. Cynthia and Julian moved out of their home and Yoko moved in, leaving her daughter in the care of her husband. While Beatles' fans around the world were ready to attack Yoko for breaking up John's marriage, it wasn't the case. Even Cynthia understood and said that Yoko provided John with the kind of support he needed.

As well as art, they made some experimental avant-garde albums together, including one called *Two Virgins*. John used a full-length nude photo of himself and Yoko that he had taken for the cover. Unfortunately, virtually no one liked the cover and they received harsh criticism for it.

A more successful venture they created was their campaign of opposition to the Vietnam War. John and Yoko planted two acorns together at Coventry Cathedral in London, representing the East (Yoko) and West (John) coming together for peace. They asked people to send two acorns to world leaders in support of the campaign, and thousands did. While the press dubbed John and Yoko "nuts for peace," the campaign was a conscience-raising success and even Israel's Golda Meir planted her acorns.

The most famous of their peace activities was their seven-day "bed-in." After their marriage in Gibraltar in 1969, John and Yoko invited reporters to join them on their honeymoon for a "peace event." While some thought they were going to be photographed making love, in fact John and Yoko did nothing but sit in bed for a week in the name of peace. Happily the event made front pages everywhere. A second bed-in was staged in Montreal, and they recorded the song "Give Peace a Chance." This song became the rallying cry at all the marches against the war that it seemed would never end.

Their work became inspirational to youths who felt helpless and uninspired. While there was much criticism, there also began to come accolades: *Rolling Stone* named Lennon "Man of the Year." But all was not well. John brought Yoko everywhere, even to recording sessions with the Beatles, who began to resent her hold on him. Finally, at the end of 1969, John had the courage to tell them what he had wanted to for a long time, that he wanted a "divorce" from the band. He wanted to pursue creating avant-garde work. While many were quick to jump on Yoko as the reason, it was John who took the blame, saying that he had "used" Yoko, which had made it easier for him to come to the decision.

Though Lennon floundered for a while after the breakup, he continued to work, and it was during this time that he recorded one of his most famous songs, "Imagine." He and Yoko moved to New York, where they bought an apartment in the famed Dakota building overlooking Central Park. Then, seemingly out of the blue, Yoko threw John out, saying she needed to be on her own for a while and not be Mrs. John Lennon. For over a year, he called her every week to ask if he could come home, and she would respond, "Not yet." Finally she agreed to date him again, and after a few months she let him back into their apartment. John told reporters, "The separation didn't work out."

In October 1975, a dream of theirs came true: Yoko gave birth to a son, Sean, on John's thirty-fifth birthday. Lennon became the father he hadn't been to Julian, and took complete care of Sean. He ran the household, baked bread, and changed diapers in complete bliss. Yoko took control of their financial affairs and through smart business deals increased their wealth to $150 million, giving 10 percent of their annual earnings to charity. At Thanksgiving they personally packed food baskets for the poor.

After five years as private citizens, John and Yoko released a statement saying that they had used the seclusion to clean their minds and think about the future, about which they were optimistic. A year later they released the album *Double Fantasy*, which contained songs that John's spirit had moved him to write after a long hiatus. On the record were a song for Sean, messages of peace, and the song "Starting Over," which is what they saw themselves as doing. Lennon offered a suggestion to the new generation: Make your dream come true.

Unfortunately, his own dream of growing old with Yoko would not come true. On December 8, 1980, Lennon was shot and killed by a deranged fan in front of his building. Yoko courageously released a statement: " 'Starting Over' still goes . . . We had talked about living until we were eighty. We even drew up lists of all the things we could do together. Then it was all over. But that doesn't mean the message is over. The music will live on."

Love on an Island Paradise

The ultimate romantic fantasy is to meet the person of your dreams and run away to live together on an island paradise, abandoning all the mundane details of daily life. Which is precisely what Elaine N. did when she met Ronald S.

The year was 1979 and the place was Leucadia, an oceanside town in Northern California. Elaine had driven cross-country and opened a health-food store called Sunflower. Since this was California in the seventies, when Elaine and her boyfriend broke up, they remained friendly, keeping the shop. Elaine, statuesque, blond, and pale-eyed, had migrated to California in search of a more laid-back lifestyle but had still retained much of her East Coast sophistication.

Shortly after breaking up with her boyfriend, Elaine was invited to a party at a cliffside house. When Elaine arrived she immediately spotted a striking man smoking a pipe. He was tall and muscular, tan, with long hair, and mesmerizing eyes. He was wearing Chinese bracelets that he had bought on his travels. To Elaine's ethereal beauty, he seemed a perfect counterbalance. Ronald, as she discovered shortly, was a wanderer. German by nationality, he had been traveling for the last ten years, since the age of seventeen. Most recently, he and the host had just returned from a boat trip up the Amazon River. Ronald and Elaine began talking.

Elaine was about to leave when Ronald confessed to her that he was desperate for a cup of coffee. He liked Leucadia and its people but found them a little too health-conscious. Elaine concurred and revealed that, even though she owned a health-food store, she had coffee in her house and that she would happily drive him there to give him some. As she returned Ronald to the party with a tin of coffee, he asked to see her again and she invited him to come to a club where she and her friends liked to dance.

They began a passionate liaison. Soon Ronald told Elaine that he was going to be leaving Leucadia to go to Tonga, a kingdom of islands in the South Pacific, where he had rented a private island. When the day of his departure arrived, Elaine drove him to the airport, and he asked her to come with him. She told him it was impossible; she had her business to think of. Ronald bought an open, first-class round-trip ticket for her and told her that if she changed her mind, his offer would still stand.

All fall Ronald wrote letters to Elaine describing the beauty of the island and the warm nature of the Tongan people. Rowing to a nearby island, he took a Polaroid of Tonga and wrote "Waiting for you" on the back, and sent it to her. As fall turned into winter, Elaine decided to join him over Christmas. The twenty-four-hour trip took her from California to Hawaii to Pago Pago in Samoa, then finally to Tonga. The Tongans had been told to expect her and when she arrived they treated her like a princess, covering her in flowers, and brought her to Ronald.

In anticipation of her arrival he had built them a house, constructed with pulleys and movable walls. Life in Tonga was slow and peaceful. "It was incredibly romantic," said Elaine. "It was hot and humid and blue all the time. A dream world." Every morning Elaine made a wood fire and cooked over it. They ate taro root, mango, and octopus, and occasionally apples from New Zealand.

After six weeks of idyllic living, Elaine and Ronald returned to the United States. In Hawaii he asked her to marry him, which she did when they returned to California. Then they packed up her things and returned to Tonga.

The Pact

In the late nineteenth century, the crown prince of the Austrian Empire did the unthinkable and entered into a suicide pact with the woman he loved and could not marry. At the age of forty, he had lived his entire life by other people's rules, and it had become unbearable. When he finally found happiness, he did not have the freedom to enjoy it. By ending his life with his true love, they were free at last.

Rudolph's father was the Emperor Francis Joseph I, a cold and domineering man who was determined to maneuver the empire and his son as he saw fit. Although the prince was given the education and training that befitted a future sovereign, the emperor had no intention of letting his exceptionally bright son have responsibilities of any kind. An early attempt of Rudolph's to share his views on his country's future was met by stony silence from his father.

At the age of twenty-two, Rudolph married Stephanie, the sixteen-year-old daughter of King Leopold of Belgium. Although a political marriage, Rudolph attempted to make it a loving one. When this failed, they drifted apart.

In October 1888, on a day at the racetrack with the visiting prince of Wales, the crown prince, then thirty, was introduced to a beautiful young woman, the Baroness Maria Vetsera. The daughter of an Austrian aristocrat and a

Greek mother, the seventeen-year-old Maria was infatuated with the handsome crown prince even before their first meeting. Not only was she prettier than the crown princess, she was more feminine and gentle. She had fallen in love with Rudolph from a distance in the spring. When her mother discovered it, she took her daughter to England for the summer to forget about him. But in the fall, back in Vienna, Maria confessed to her governess that she loved him still. As her family had not been introduced at court, her chances of meeting the crown prince socially were next to none. She schemed a way to meet him without her family knowing.

It turned out that the prince's first cousin Marie Larisch was one of Maria's best friends. Through Marie, Maria arranged to have herself brought to the prince's bachelor quarters in November. While nothing happened at that meeting except a friendly conversation, soon they were exchanging letters through Rudolph's valet and Maria's maid. By December, the Vienna opera was performing a cycle of Wagner operas, and while Maria's mother and sister attended, Maria begged off with a different excuse each time. As soon as they were gone, she would visit with Rudolph for the duration of the opera. To her governess she wrote, "He is my god, my everything!" The feeling was becoming increasingly mutual on the prince's part, who wrote to her that he could not live without her.

Maria was so many things that Stephanie was not. She loved him wholly and passionately; she listened when he spoke to her of his troubles. She had an instinct to know what Rudolph needed. As a gift he gave her an iron wedding ring, which she wore on a chain around her neck. On it was engraved the initials for the German words "United in Love Till Death." Maria wrote to her governess that they had made a suicide pact, in which they would kill themselves after spending a few happy hours together.

Rudolph made plans with two friends to go to Mayerling, south of Vienna, where he had his hunting lodge, on January 28. Although he had been expected back at an imperial family dinner the next night, he begged off, claiming illness. That evening he dined with a friend and then, professing illness again, retired early to his room, where Maria awaited him.

With the help of Marie Larisch, Maria had left home under the guise of going shopping. In fact, Marie's son-in-law drove Maria to Mayerling, where she stayed with Rudolph. To cover her tracks, Marie went to the police saying that the girl had disappeared and that she was concerned that she was with the crown prince and might commit suicide, as she had found a letter to that effect. The police hesitated to act because the relationship with Maria was unknown to them and they were reluctant to disturb His Highness. By the time they decided to get involved, the next day, at the urging of Maria's mother, it was too late.

After dinner with his friend, Rudolph returned to his room and Maria. They drank wine and he had his faithful coachman come into the bedroom and sing some sentimental Viennese songs for them. After the servant finished performing the songs they loved so much, Maria wrote her farewell letters to her family. To her sister, she wrote, "We are both going blissfully into the uncertain beyond. Think of me now and then. Be happy and marry only for love. I could not do it and since I could not resist love, I am going with him . . . Do not weep for my sake. I am crossing the line merrily. It is so beautiful out here . . . Again farewell."

Rudolph had written his farewell letters in Vienna, including one to his mother in which he asked to be buried beside the "pure angel who accompanied me into the other world." He and Maria discussed how to end their lives, by revolver or poison, deciding on the gun. She lay on the bed and he pulled the trigger, ending her young life. Next, instead of immediately following, he waited. He unlocked his door and told his faithful servant to prepare his breakfast. Then he returned to the bedroom. He placed a rose in Maria's hands. Using a hand mirror to locate the correct spot on his temple, he placed the gun against it and pulled the trigger.

"Good Night, Gracie"

There is no doubt that Gracie Allen was the best thing to ever happen to George Burns. Both vaudeville performers, they hooked up as a team in 1923, when Allen was just eighteen. Burns was looking for a "straight man" to feed him the lines to which he would deliver a funny response. Only in the Burns-Allen act it never happened that way. Gracie was such a natural comedienne that the audience laughed the moment she spoke, before Burns could even deliver his line. The dizzy character Gracie Allen was such a hit that all Burns had to do was stand there. Eventually he decided to smoke a cigar onstage so he would have something to do.

Slowly Burns fell madly in love with his partner. But the young Allen loved another performer, Benny Ryan, whom she was set on marrying. Charming, handsome, and Irish like Gracie, Ryan had a flaw that Burns did not: He was undependable. Burns, on the other hand, was always right there by Allen's side whenever she needed him. Of course, he needed her: She was their meal ticket.

After a year of being in love with Gracie, George finally decided to tell her. She laughed at him and he didn't mention it again for a while. Their popularity was growing and in two years they had gone from being "dissies"—the disappointment act that fills in when the real act cancels—to playing in decent theaters. Still, Gracie had her heart set on marrying Benny Ryan.

She was about to quit when the Burns-Allen act landed a guaranteed sixteen-week engagement for the Orpheum tour. It had always been Gracie's dream to see her picture in the lobby of the San Francisco Orpheum, the theater she had spent so many afternoons in as a child. Also, the tour paid $450 a week, so Gracie agreed to go there instead of to New York to marry Benny. She had a last stipulation for George: If they were going to be making a transcontinental trip, she needed a steamer trunk, which George carried home on his back through a snowstorm for her.

It was during that trip that George seriously asked Gracie to marry him. In his biography of Gracie, he wrote:

> I'll never forget her response: if I could have gotten that kind of laughter from an audience, I would have been successful years earlier. I even bought a ring. It sold for $35 but I managed to

get it for $20. It was a very special ring—the metal band actually changed colors as it aged in my pocket.

Gracie turned him down, saying she wanted security when she married, and the successful Benny Ryan represented that for her. When Burns and Allen reached the last stop on the tour, San Francisco, Allen had to be rushed to the hospital with a case of appendicitis. Knowing how much Gracie loved flowers, Burns borrowed two hundred dollars from her and filled her hospital room with them. She asked him to wire Benny Ryan to let him know what had happened. Because he was broke and didn't want Gracie to know—and because he couldn't bear to let Ryan have her—George never sent the wire. Gracie was heartbroken that Benny had let her down.

When they returned to New York, Benny Ryan was out of town, but Burns was miserable because Gracie was planning to marry him anyway. Twenty-dollar ring in hand, George pressed her again, to no avail. That Christmas Eve, they went to a small party thrown by a close friend to exchange gifts. When George opened the card on his from Gracie, he read what she had written aloud, "To Nattie, with all my love." Burns laughed out loud and said, "All your love? Ha, ha, ha. You don't even know what love means." Gracie left the room in tears.

She had planned to call Benny Ryan at midnight to wish him a merry Christmas, but didn't. When he called her several hours later to ask why she hadn't called, she told him she didn't love him anymore. She called George at three in the morning and told him, "You can buy the wedding ring if you want to."

When he asked her why she had changed her mind,

she told him that he was the only boy who had ever made her cry, and she decided that if he could make her cry, she must really love him. She wore her twenty-dollar wedding ring until the day she died.

Burns and Allen went on to be more successful than they ever imagined. They graduated to having their own shows on radio, then went into films, and television. Their career together spanned thirty years, until Gracie, who had been asking to retire for several years, finally got her way. She wanted to spend more time with her children and grandchildren and she had developed a heart condition. Six years after leaving show business without ever looking back, Gracie unexpectedly dropped in on the set of the television show George and their son Ronnie were working on to have lunch with them. She received a standing ovation from the crew. The following evening, while watching television, she called out for George's help. Several hours later, her heart gave out.

People often asked Burns if he was jealous of his wife's success. No, he said, in thirty-eight years of marriage, they were never competitive with each other. As George wrote, "Gracie got the laughs, and at the end of the night, I got to bring Gracie home."

The Showgirl

Until one fateful evening, Jack S. knew exactly what his life was going to be like: comfortable, but not all that exciting. A well-to-do New York businessman with interests in real estate and the garment industry, Jack not only worked with his brother but the two were also married to women who were sisters. The two couples did everything together.

One evening in the early 1930s, the foursome went out to see Eddie Cantor and the Ziegfeld Follies, the hottest ticket around. The star act of the show was a young flamenco dancer who Ziegfeld had billed as "The Most Beautiful Woman in the World."

The moment sixteen-year-old Trini emerged onto the stage and began to dance, Jack was totally smitten. Never in his life had he ever felt the way he felt at that moment. All he knew was that he was in love.

Every day Jack sent Trini huge bouquets of flowers. Every night he went to the show and waited for her after each performance. Slowly he was able to meet her and eventually was able to take her out for supper—chaperoned, of course. For the raven-haired teenager from Seville, her thirty-year-old suitor seemed strange. Culturally, the two could not have been farther apart, since Trini was a devout Catholic and spoke no English and Jack was Jewish and didn't speak a word of Spanish. Needless to say, that he was married further complicated the situation.

After several months, Trini decided to go home for a visit. Without telling Jack, she booked a passage on an ocean liner heading for Spain. The day the ship was to sail, Jack heard of her plans. He rushed to a jeweler and bought a diamond engagement ring and raced to the port. He was too late. The cruise ship had left the port and was heading out of New York Harbor. With not a moment to waste, Jack hired a motor boat to take him to the ocean liner. They sped down the Hudson River until they reached the ship, and Jack was given permission to board.

The whole trip across the ocean, Jack courted Trini, who remained unconvinced. Once in Spain, he accompanied her to her family's home. Upon meeting Trini's parents, Jack poured out his heart to them. He told them how much he loved their daughter, that he was getting divorced and wanted to marry Trini. If only they would give their permission and help him convince Trini to marry him. Trini's parents were moved by Jack's pleas and agreed to help him. Trini finally gave in and accepted his proposal. Jack effected a divorce from his wife, which fortunately was so amicable that they all attended family gatherings together after their remarriages (they were, of course, still related through the marriage of Jack's brother and her sister). After Jack and Trini were married, she gave up the showgirl life and for ten months a year was a dedicated—and very stylish—Jewish housewife. For the other two months a year, when she and Jack went to Spain to visit her parents and sisters, she was Catholic. It worked beautifully, for over thirty years.

Above the Clouds

The romance between the famed flyer Charles Lindbergh and the writer Anne Morrow was one that was born flying high above the clouds and out of the public eye. They met shortly after he made his 1927 record-breaking flight from New York to Paris, when her father, the United States ambassador to Mexico, invited him south of the border to help ease Mexican-American relations. Lindbergh admired

Dwight Morrow, and happy to get out of the limelight, he spent Christmas with the Morrow family.

Although the handsome and charming Charles was the most sought-after bachelor in the world, Anne had viewed him as a heroic figure, but could not comprehend why throngs of women followed him wherever he went. The moment Charles shook Anne's hand on the receiving line at the embassy, however, she understood. Anne knew at that moment that her life was forever changed and she dreamed of a life with him.

Their first meeting was not as memorable for Charles, however, who initially was taken with Anne's older sister Elizabeth. Fortunately, the relationship didn't last, and one afternoon in October 1928, when Charles telephoned to the Morrows' New York City apartment looking for Dwight, Anne was surprised but thrilled when Charles invited her to go flying with him. Since the press would have them immediately "engaged" if he took her to an airfield near the city, he drove her out to the Guggenheim Estate at Sands Point and took off from the private landing strip there. They soared over New York and New Jersey and Anne discovered to her amazement that she was enthralled with flying.

When news of the romance leaked out, the embassy firmly denied it. But by February 1929, the embassy released a statement announcing the engagement. Anne was deliriously happy, but still could not believe that she was to marry Charles.

In May, upon the return of Charles's mother from a teaching post abroad, the Morrow family invited their closest friends to a party in her honor. It was not until the guests saw the Morrow family minister and Charles next to him in a suit that they realized that this was to be

Charles's wedding day. After a quick ceremony, the couple changed clothes and drove out past the unsuspecting reporters. For once in his life, Charles had pulled one over on the press.

After the initial excitement of her marriage died down, Anne settled into her new role as Charles's wife. For the serious former Smith College student, whose passion above all was literature, she considered Charles her intellectual inferior. He knew nothing of the great books and spoke no foreign languages. Still, she underestimated Charles, who, unlike most men of the time, expected his wife to be his equal. That included being his flying partner. Luckily she was mad about it and quickly learned how to be a member of the crew of a plane. This included working a radio, becoming touch-perfect in Morse code, learning to read charts, and most important being a co-pilot in the event that anything happened to her husband while they were aloft. Charles was relentless in his quest for perfection, forcing Anne to perform landings over and over again until she got it just right. By the middle of their first year of marriage, seven months pregnant, she was his copilot on his fourteen-hour record-breaking flight across the United States.

Anne discovered that while Charles might not know much about literature, he had a wealth of knowledge to teach her. He was interested in many things that she had never considered, such as science, space, animals, and nature. Ashamed she had ever entertained snobbish thoughts, Anne decided her love of books and writing would be the one thing she would keep just for herself.

Their life together survived the most horrible tragedy parents can face: the kidnapping of their first child, Charles, in March 1932. After the infant was found dead seventy-two days later, Charles became obsessed with solving the crime. Anne, pregnant again, was more resolved to letting go, but Charles could not. He believed that publicity had killed his baby and appealed to the public after the birth of their second child, Jon, to let his family live in private.

Eventually the Lindberghs left America for the relative calm of England. Unfortunately, Charles, impressed by the Germans' air power, grew to believe that Hitler could win World War II. After moving back to the United States, he urged America not to get involved in the war, a stance that made him even more unpopular after the Japanese bombed Pearl Harbor. Eventually he flew for the U.S. Air Force against the Japanese, after much persuading of the top military brass. Anne privately disagreed with Charles's views on the Germans, but publicly supported him and even suggested that his opinions were misunderstood. It was an extremely difficult time for her, now the mother of four young children, to have the public sentiment have come full circle to be so anti-Lindbergh.

Over the years, Anne had commenced a writing career that had been quite successful, especially for so busy a woman. She wrote poetry, memoirs, and essays, and her book *A Gift from the Sea*, a meditation on getting away from it all and living simply, became a bestseller and remains a classic today.

In their golden years, Anne and Charles became committed ecologists, as well as doting grandparents. They still traveled nonstop, Anne to see her children, who were spread over the world, and Charles because he could not help it. When he was diagnosed with advanced lymphatic cancer at the age of seventy-two, he prepared for his death as he prepared for all journeys. Having decided he would not die in bed but somewhere beautiful, he insisted on being flown to Maui. By the sea and in the sun he lingered for ten days as he planned his funeral. His last act before he closed his eyes for the last time was to say good-bye to his beloved wife and partner.

The Shipboard Romance

It was the spring of 1952 and twenty-year-old Phyllis Culberston, a Smith College student, was engaged to marry a man whom her father did not care for at all. There was nothing particularly wrong with Phyllis's fiancé, but he lacked the character that Phyllis's parents had hoped her husband would have. So as a graduation present to Phyllis's older sister Patty—and as an excuse to get Phyllis out of town—her father sent the sisters on a transatlantic cruise and a tour of Europe.

Also crossing the ocean was twenty-four-year-old Bill Draper, who had just come back from Korea and was to return to Yale that fall. His father, a four-star general and the roving ambassador to NATO, was in Europe and had given the cruise as a gift to his son. A friend of his who knew the Culberston sisters told Bill to seek out Phyllis on the ship, describing her as "a neat package."

Their first day on the ship, the sisters and Bill discovered one another on line to sign up for what they thought was dinner but what turned out to be deck chairs. After Bill introduced himself, Phyllis immediately suggested he join them at dinner, thinking he would be perfect for Patty. By the second day, Phyllis decided that she wasn't sure she wanted Patty to have him and thought that she might want him for herself. On the third day Bill kissed her and said, "Instead of kissing that other guy in June why don't you marry me?"

To her own surprise, Phyllis didn't say no. It was quickly dawning on her that she could not marry her fiancé regardless of what was to happen with Bill. She phoned her parents for their advice. Her mother, a renowned beauty, told her, "Oh it's just a shipboard romance; I've had many of them in my day." But her father was more specific. He said he was happy she was breaking off the engagement but that he had done some research on Bill Draper and that "he seems to have a reputation as a bounder." Undaunted, Phyllis called her fiancé, broke up with him, and spent the rest of the cruise on the deck chair next to Bill. One day while they were sunbathing, she noticed two large scars on his side and back and asked him about them. A quick-thinking Bill answered that it was a war wound, that a bullet had entered in on his side and had gone through his back. At that moment Phyllis fell instantly in love with him. Only ten years later did Bill confess that they were boil scars and that had a bullet really traveled that path it would have gone directly through his heart.

The young lovers parted company in London and Bill went on to Paris. After several days he missed Phyllis so much he called her to say that he wanted to meet up with her at her next stop, Brussels. For the next month he visited her in Rome, Naples, Capri, and Lucerne, abandoning his original plans to visit his parents. Finally they met again in Paris on what was to be their last night in

Europe. It was Phyllis's birthday and Bill took her to a romantic restaurant, where the staff caught wind of a cause for celebration, sending over champagne and strolling violin players. It was only when the check arrived that Bill discovered that these added items were not free. They scraped together all their money, finding between them barely enough to pay the check. On the way out, the maître d' and his staff were lined up, hands outstretched, so Bill and Phyllis emptied their pockets of all the foreign currency they had accumulated. By the time they got into a cab, they realized they only had enough money to get back to Phyllis's hotel. It was too late to take the Metro. Bill, Phyllis, and Patty stayed up all night talking, and at six in the morning they were startled by the phone ringing. It was Bill's father, asking if his son was there, to which she embarrassedly said yes.

The Drapers returned to the States with Bill and the Culbertson sisters on the *Rhyndam* that day. With Phyllis's ex-fiancé calling constantly, she was a wreck, unable to decide whether to marry Bill. Finally Bill assured her there were other fish in the ocean and she snapped out of it. Forty-four years later they are still together, and among many other things they produced the marvelous actress Polly Draper.

I Gotta Horse Right Here . . .

One of the most remarkable sights one can see in New York City is a mounted police officer. He seems an anomaly as he rides his horse slowly through the bustling, noisy traffic of the city, a kind of calming force. Officer Steve G. had the good luck to be posted in front of Rockefeller Center and to be riding a gorgeous chestnut named Fabian. Every day a young woman named Felina R. passed by him at his midtown post and stopped to pet Fabian.

"I couldn't take my eyes off him," Felina said. She didn't mean Steve, who as a six-foot-two Irishman wasn't rough on the eyes either. But for a while, Felina only had eyes for Fabian.

Soon she realized that Steve seemed to be particularly nice to her and certainly a good deal friendlier to her than most of the other mounted officers stationed there. She began to look forward to seeing him each day. Still, Steve wore an Irish friendship ring on the ring finger of his right hand, so Felina thought perhaps he was involved or married. One day, she gathered up her courage.

"I'll bet your children love that you work with a horse," she ventured. Steve had a deadpan expression on his face.

"I'm not married," said Steve. Felina tried not to smile. At that moment began a fairy-tale New York romance.

For their first date, Steve took Felina to the Rainbow Room, high atop Rockefeller Center. As they danced on the revolving floor that gave a 360-degree view of the city, Felina realized that she could get serious about this man.

They began dating, as Felina went through a career change. She traded in her wholesale job for a stint at Legal Aid. After a year there, the Police Department called. Felina had taken the police exam four years earlier, and all of a sudden was being given six hours to decide whether she wanted to join the new class of recruits at the Police Academy the following week. She signed up and became an officer.

Meanwhile, Steve was rising through the ranks, having been promoted to sergeant. In September, on their way to a wedding, he took Felina to the Palm Court of the Plaza Hotel and proposed. Then he began studying for his lieutenant's exam.

Steve and Felina were both so busy with their jobs that they weren't doing much wedding planning. One snowy January day, Felina was waiting at the bus stop with an elderly neighbor. When the bus didn't come and the older woman began to walk, Felina offered to walk with her. As they talked, Felina mentioned she was engaged, and the neighbor told her she had read in the paper about an essay contest to win a fifty-thousand-dollar wedding at the Rainbow Room on Valentine's Day. After hearing that Felina had done no wedding plan at all, she strongly suggested Felina enter the contest.

Felina read the rules and sat down to write her essay. She wrote about how she had fallen in love with Fabian and then Steve on the street right in front of Rockefeller Center. She mentioned that now they both worked for the

NYPD. At the end she asked if they thought that Fabian would fit in the elevator up to the Rainbow Room.

Several weeks later, on January 30, Steve and Felina got a call telling them they were among five finalists. As they held hands, dressed in their best clothes, walking to the street where they had met, Felina said to Steve, "Even if we don't win, isn't this a great thing to tell the grandkids?" When they got upstairs the executives from the Rainbow Room told them they had a surprise for them: They were the winners. Then they were brought downstairs to be introduced to the media. As it happened, the mayor of New York, Rudolph Giuliani, was emerging from a meeting in the building and was in the lobby. So with Steve and Felina's permission, the people from the Rainbow Room put him on the spot, asking if he would marry them on Valentine's Day. He said that he would be honored.

The next two weeks were a whirlwind of activity, as wedding preparations were hastily made. Finally Valentine's Day came and their forty guests were escorted into the building by an honor guard of mounted officers from Steve's unit. (Unfortunately Fabian wasn't able to be there; he was recovering from injuries he received when he and Steve were hit by a drunk driver on New Year's Eve.) The couple immediately went back to work—delaying the eight-day honeymoon in Jamaica they had also won—since Steve had to study for the lieutenant's exam.

He passed and was put on the list for promotion. And Felina, who finished up at the Midtown Precinct, which covers Rockefeller Center, got news of her new post: the Mounted Unit.

Revolutionary Love

The bride's father described it as "the marriage between an elephant and a dove," but when twenty-year-old Frida Kahlo wed the great painter Diego Rivera a dream of seven years came true. They first met when Rivera came to Kahlo's Mexico City prep school to paint a mural. The delicate but striking fifteen-year-old took one look at the two-hundred-pound artist with the bulging eyes and told a friend, "My ambition is to have a child by Diego Rivera."

Although she tried as hard as she could to get the thirty-six-year-old painter's attention, her schoolgirl tricks of playing pranks on him and calling him names met with no success. Although he was far from handsome, Rivera was charming, brilliant, and did not suffer from a lack of women. A revolutionary, his art was often political and had made him a celebrity in his native Mexico.

A short time after meeting Rivera, Kahlo was severely injured in a school bus accident that broke her spine, collarbone, pelvis, and right leg, and crushed her right foot. Spending months in a body cast, she asked for paint and canvas as a way to pass the time. Kahlo devoted herself seriously to painting after the accident. While she had recovered enough to regain mobility, she now walked with a profound limp as a result of her injured right leg. More significant were the emotional changes that had taken place and that were reflected in the haunting self-portraits that became her hallmark.

Several years passed, until one day Kahlo sought out Rivera at the Ministry of Education, where he was painting another mural. She asked him to come down from his scaffold to critique a painting she had brought to show him. She wanted to know if he thought she might be able to make a living as an artist. Rivera was impressed with her work, and after finishing the mural he began to pursue the young painter.

They shared political convictions as well as intellectual ones, and for the first time Rivera felt that he had met his equal in all ways. They married in 1929 and began a life together devoted to art. Kahlo tried to attain her goal of bearing Rivera's child but after two miscarriages, probably as a result of her injured pelvis, was unable to. Rivera's fame became worldwide and soon he returned to his womanizing ways. Although she tried to look the other way, Kahlo could not and eventually began to have affairs of her own. Eventually, in 1939, the couple divorced.

In spite of the end of their marriage, Rivera and Kahlo knew they were each other's soul mates and Rivera was still very much in love with her. Under the pretense of taking her to see a bone surgeon, Rivera organized a reunion a year later. The couple soon remarried and remained together until her death in 1954.

Duet

The opera world's current sensation is not one rising star, but two, whose singing together is electrifying opera fans everywhere because of their real-life romance. The tenor Roberto Alagna and the soprano Angela Gheorghiu met in 1992 at London's Covent Garden when they were both in *La Bohème*. For the thirty-two-year-old Alagna, the opera was a strange example of life imitating art. On stage in *La Bohème*, Mimi expires from consumption; in reality, Alagna's wife was dying of a brain tumor, leaving him with a young daughter.

For Gheorghiu and Alagna, there were no instant fireworks but a mutual understanding they saw in each other's eyes. The thirty-year-old soprano first took the opera world by storm when she made her debut—not in some small theater or on tour, but in *La Traviata* at Covent Garden. Gheorghiu is a classic beauty: reed thin, with black hair and milky skin.

Alagna, born in France to a Sicilian father, took a more circuitous route to the opera stage. Wanting to be a pop singer, he spent years singing in a cabaret. Through a mentor who was an opera buff, he studied technique by listening to the friend's records. Then he entered the voice competition sponsored by the star who critics say he is destined to replace, Luciano Pavarotti, and won. Soon he was on stage at La Scala. Like Gheorghiu, Alagna has a charismatic onstage presence. With a reddish beard, he is handsome, exuding virility and warmth.

The two have been virtually inseparable since getting together after the first performance of *La Bohème*. Shortly after Alagna's debut at the Met, in April 1996, the two were married. For audiences, it is a dream come true to know that the electricity between them onstage is real. Finally the opera world has its own first couple. It is their desire to work together as much as possible, because, as Alagna described, together they are "invincible."

"A Cup of Coffee, a Sandwich, and You"

David C., a Long Island bagel store manager, knew he had met the woman of his dreams when Laura S. walked into his shop and ordered a coffee one morning last year. In fact, he was so confident of it that he assured his co-worker Tina that not only would he get Laura to go out with him but that he would marry her. Tina, whose boyfriend was friends with Laura's boyfriend, told him that not only was he dreaming, but that Laura's boyfriend would break his legs if he found out David liked her.

Every morning Laura, a blue-eyed blonde who owned a hairdressing salon around the corner, would come to the bagel shop and, as she was on Weight Watchers, just order coffee. David would politely serve her, always telling her to have a nice day or that he would see her later, but Laura never paid any attention to him. Usually she would chat with Tina for a little while about how the two of them were going to get rid of their good-for-nothing boyfriends. Unbeknownst to Laura, David always listened to them behind a partition.

One night Laura and her boyfriend had an enormous fight and broke up. The next morning she went to the bagel shop and told Tina about it while David, hiding behind a wall, listened in. When he came out front Laura asked him to make her a ham, cheese, and egg sandwich. "And make the eggs over easy," she ordered. David didn't seem to be paying close attention to her request, she thought, but she didn't say anything. When she got to the salon and opened up her sandwich, she discovered that it was well-done and covered in ketchup, not what she had ordered at all. Furious, she stormed back to the shop and threw her sandwich at David's face. He began laughing; his plan to get her to notice him had worked. He apologized and went back to the kitchen to make her another.

A few days later, Laura came into the shop holding a Bingo scratch-off card on which she had won twelve dollars. David had won a hundred and fifty dollars bowling the night before. "Let's spend it together," he said. Laura turned him down, saying that she couldn't because she had just broken up with her boyfriend. He told her he would give her time. After a month and a half of hinting, David invited Laura to come watch him in a bowling tournament. Afterward he took her out to dinner. A week later she went to the movies with him and then left for a vacation in Florida, where she discovered to her amazement that she was thinking about him. She called. He was shocked. When she arrived back to work her first day back there was an enormous bouquet of flowers, "So big it covered my whole station."

Two months later, David showed up at the salon and dragged her into the supply closet, much to the surprise of her mother and the clients. He got down on one knee, gave Laura a ring, and proposed.

The Loves of the Saints

During the Middle Ages a young Italian noble girl fell in love with a merchant's son who was dedicating his life to God. Deciding she must follow in his path, the young woman gave up her worldly possessions and devoted herself to his philosophy of redemption through absolute poverty. Their holy lives and partnership inspired thousands of followers and resulted in the sainthoods of St. Francis and St. Clare.

The eighteen-year-old Clare was a beautiful, blond-haired daughter of one of the most noble families in Assisi. As the age of marriage was upon her, her family presented her with many young aristocratic men from whom to choose a husband, but Clare was not interested. She preferred Francis, the son of a merchant and thus of a much lower class. All of Assisi knew of Francis, who had refused to enter his father's successful profession and who preferred the company of lepers to gentlemen.

This greatly intrigued young Clare, who, coming upon him one day in the street, spoke to him.

To Clare, Francis said just, "You will have to know how to die."

"What do you mean?" asked Clare.

"On the cross with Christ."

Clare attended Palm Sunday services and at the moment that the hosannas of the liturgy were being read, decided she would "die," as Francis had told her to. That evening Clare left her life in Assisi behind. In all Italian homes of the time, there existed two doors: the main door of the house and a door that was only for the dead, who had to exit it feet first. If one left through this door it meant that one was irrevocably separated from one's family and never returning. The newly "dead" Clare jumped out this door and ran to the woods where Francis's men were waiting for her.

The men took Clare to the tiny chapel where Francis waited for her. There he stripped her of her jewelry and embroidered dress and gave her a coarse habit to wear. Then Francis took a razor to her long blond hair and cut it off, covering her head with a woolen cloth. Then he took her to a nearby monastery and into the care of nuns, where no one could reach her.

When her family heard what Clare had done, they were furious and especially so at Francis. Her mother sent her brother to bring her home, but Clare would only see him in the chapel. As she was touching the altar when he approached her—an act so holy that no violence was permitted as it was done—he was not able to do more than look at her.

Francis, while at the altar of a nearby church called St. Damian's, heard a voice that told him to repair the church, which was nearly in ruins. After doing so, Francis came to understand the intention was not just for a material repair but a spiritual one as well. He installed Clare in the empty church, where she began an order at St. Damian's called the Ladies of Poverty. The women went barefoot, wore threadbare garments, and ate only stale bread, but they lived to help the worst-off. Clare was never happier than when she espoused Francis's theology of poverty and tended to the sickest people. Soon many of the young noble women renounced their wealth and joined Clare and her Ladies of Poverty.

Though Francis was reluctant to spend time with her because he did not believe he should be seen coming and going from the church, Clare finally convinced him that they should share a meal. Francis permitted her to leave the church one day to have a picnic with him in the woods. Legend has it that as they sat and Francis began to speak of his love of the Lord, there emanated a light from the two of them that grew so bright it glowed more strongly than the sun and could be seen by the townsfolk of Assisi. They gathered around to see Francis and Clare rapt in ecstasy and seemingly haloed in the glow.

From then on, Francis came from time to time to see Clare at St. Damian's—which he had forbidden her to leave—to give her the emotional and spiritual nourishment she needed to continue. At the end of Francis's life, his followers brought his broken body to St. Damian's for Clare to see him before he died. She kissed his wounds before they took him to his resting place.

The sainted Francis was buried in the church of St. George, but the townspeople of Assisi worried that the church was too open and that the treasured body might be stolen. Later the body was moved to the newly built basilica, which was like a fortress. After Clare's death, her body lay at St. Damian's under constant guard by Assisi's soldiers. After St. Francis's body was moved to the basilica, St. Clare's was moved to the church of St. George. A basilica was placed on top of it and the church was renamed the Basilica of St. Clare. As she had in life, Clare followed Francis in death. Just a few blocks apart, the saints' resting places now draw thousands of visitors each year.

Nick and Nora

The relationship between Dashiell Hammett and Lillian Hellman could hardly be described as traditionally romantic, but the creator of Sam Spade and one of this century's most notable playwrights were at their best when they were together.

Hammett was the country's most popular detective-fiction writer when he met the young Hellman in 1930. Dash had been put on retainer by one of the big movie studios at a time when gangster pictures were all the rage. Hollywood was a fantasy world, and during his years there Hammett lived fast, boozing, gambling, and womanizing. On a five-day bender and in desperate need of someone to talk to, he met Hellman in a Los Angeles restaurant. She joined him for a drink and they wound up talking all night. Hellman was unhappy, having recently come to the realization that she wanted to write, and was drowning her sorrows because her job reading movie scripts was making her miserable.

The love affair blossomed in spite of her husband,

who soon gallantly relinquished her and befriended Hammett, and in spite of Hammett's constant extracurricular dalliances. But Dashiell realized that the quick-witted Lillian meant a great deal more to him than any of the starlets and barmaids he was bedding. When Hellman took a trip to New York soon after their relationship began, in typical Hammett style, he wrote to her, "The emptiness I thought was hunger for chow mein turned out to be for you." They were both too cynical to play lovebirds.

Hammett was determined to help Hellman write, and when she decided it would be plays, he suggested the topic for her first one. A harsh critic, Dashiell believed a writer's work must be really good; if it wasn't, it shouldn't be published. He went over every word Lillian wrote and told her to study writing just as he had, by reading and writing constantly. As a result of his tutoring, Lillian's first effort was bought by a producer immediately. The play *The Children's Hour* opened in New York in 1934 to rave reviews. When she called Dash in Los Angeles to let him know, however, a woman answered the phone claiming to be Hammett's "secretary." Enraged, Lillian got on a plane to the Coast, let herself into the house, smashed his basement ice cream parlor to pieces, and flew back to New York.

At the time, Hammett was working on his screenplay for *The Thin Man*. William Powell played a retired detective named Nick Charles, whose wisecracking wife Nora is always urging him back into the business. Dashiell didn't have to look far for the basis of these characters: They were Lillian and him. Hammett had been a Pinkerton detective before he began writing and, like Nick, was a stylish dresser. *The Thin Man* and its subsequent sequels were huge hits. Hammett put aside the novel he was working on and never went back to writing fiction. After a particularly long binge of debauched living in Hollywood, he was put on a plane back to New York and Hellman, who nursed him back to health. She bought 130 acres in Westchester, which they named Hardscrabble Farm, and the two of them relished their roles as gentleman farmers. Hammett helped her with her next play, *The Little Foxes*, another hit.

Hammett continued writing his screenplays and living large and Hellman worked on her plays. Living apart as they did, Dash would eventually burn out and be sent back to Lillian, who always nursed him back to health. Finally she had enough, and when called again to his side in 1948 she said no. Hammett's housekeeper pleaded with her until she came. Dash was trembling and convulsing. Lillian took him to a hospital, where a doctor told him that if he didn't quit drinking he would die. He stopped.

Hammett quit writing and got involved in Communist Party political causes, even going to jail for six months for contempt of court when he refused to answer questions about an organization with which he was involved. Hellman also faced the McCarthy hearings, but was never charged. The IRS came down hard on both of them, and Hellman was forced to sell their beloved Hardscrabble Farm. Dash too was broke, and for the first time in their lives they lived together. Several years later he was diagnosed with cancer. As she always had been when he needed her, Lillian was by his side when he died.

Happily Ever After

Joseph M. and Patrick L. never set out to change the world. Rather, one morning, after being together every day for ten years, they set out for City Hall to do what they always wanted to do: get married. Little did they know that their simple desire would lead to a six-year legal battle or would become a major issue in the 1996 presidential campaign.

Joseph and Pat are each other's perfect mates. Both Hawaii residents, they met when Joseph was helping to teach disco dancing to senior citizens. The class teacher heard of a new dance called Le Freak and had gone to a nightclub to recruit someone to teach it to his students. When Pat walked through the dance studio door to teach the dance, it was love at first sight for Joseph and him. They went out after class and have been together ever since.

Immediately they discovered that they had much in common. In fact, some of the similarities are downright bizarre: Both have a father and brother named Fred and a sister named Barbara Jean. Both of their fathers were life-long employees of the U.S. Postal Service and both sets of parents got married on the bride's birthday. More important to Pat and Joseph were their strict Catholic upbringing, which invested them with a sense of commitment—and ceremony.

Joseph was already running a small catering business

at the time. Pat's talents lay in flower arranging and sewing, so the couple created a company called Gourmet Associates and Design that puts on weddings, funerals, bar mitzvahs, and the like, doing everything from food, flowers, fashion, and design to making an event happen. For them, a wedding was a natural.

What Pat and Joseph discovered when they got to City Hall was that there was no law against same-sex marriages—the legal terminology speaks only of spouses—but that no one would perform the ceremony.

Anticipating a struggle ahead, Joseph and Pat hired a civil rights attorney. In May 1993, the Supreme Court of the state of Hawaii ruled that the couple had the legal right to marry. The court also ruled, however, that the state could file an appeal if it could come up with a good reason why same-sex marriages should be prevented. The filing of the appeal effectively froze the Supreme Court's decision, making it impossible for Pat and Joseph to wed, and for the last few years, the state has continually asked for extensions of the appeal as it prepares its case.

If the state's appeal is turned down, Pat and Joseph know exactly what they will do: immediately get married either in a judge's chambers or by a justice of the peace. They will do this because the state will probably file a stay preventing same-sex marriages. Pat and Joseph intend to beat them to the punch. Then they will have the Hawaiian-style wedding celebration they have always dreamed of.

For this couple, who have been together nineteen years, the last six have been trying. Now recognized nearly everywhere they go, their private life has gone under a magnifying glass. Still, they have no regrets for the great stride forward their act of love has made for gays and lesbians. Joseph believes they have helped people in the United States learn more about them: "That we're everyday people and that we too can fall in love. It is a simple matter of falling in love."

And getting married. And living happily ever after.

The Jazz Age's Perfect Couple

The famed 1920s American expatriates Sara and Gerald Murphy were a couple who found refuge and happiness in France but also in their love for each other. Members of the intellectual and artistic elite of twenties Modernism, the Murphys' lives were charmed, and their friends were irresistibly drawn to them. So inspiring was this twosome that they became models for their famed friends': Sara was painted by Picasso and F. Scott Fitzgerald modeled *Tender Is the Night*'s Dick Diver in part on Gerald.

Their romance began as a friendship among teenagers, a consequence of Gerald's pouring out his sad heart in letters to a girl willing to really listen, Sara Wiborg. The son of the owner of an upscale leather-goods company in New York, Gerald was expected to work in the family business. After doing so for several restless years, Gerald confided his unhappiness to Sara. One of his chief complaints was that he had no outlet through which to discuss his love of art and books, for fear of being thought effeminate. Sara, who had been raised primarily in Europe and was a great beauty of the day, lent Murphy her ear and eventually her heart.

In 1915 they married. After short stints by Gerald in the army and graduate school in landscape architecture, the Murphys and their children moved to Paris in 1921. There, Gerald was mesmerized by the art he saw. The Cubists—such as Braque, Cézanne, and Picasso—inspired him to try his own hand at painting, which he did over the next seven years. Although he produced only ten paintings, they were noteworthy as precursors to the Pop movement. Three remain today in the collections of the Museum of Modern Art and the Dallas Museum for Contemporary Art.

But it was hardly Gerald's painting for which the Murphys were known. Rather it was their art for living. The family moved from Paris to the South of France, where they built a home they named the Villa America. Sara was a wonderful hostess to an amazing array of visitors, including Gertrude Stein and Alice B. Toklas, Picasso, Zelda and F. Scott Fitzgerald, Cole Porter (a classmate of Gerald's from Yale who had brought him to the Riviera), John Dos Passos, Fernand Léger, and many more. To be at the Villa America in its beautiful, fragrant gardens, looking out over the wonder and eating Sara's delicious food, was heaven.

The elegant Murphys also set the style wherever they were. Gerald, who was a bit of a dandy, adopted the French sailor uniform of striped shirts, white pants, and caps, making it popular beachwear. Sara wore loose flowing clothes and her hair in a long braid until she bobbed it in the style of the day. She also had a habit of wearing a strand of pearls slung down her back at the beach because it was "good for them to get the sun." This image appears in some of Picasso's paintings of women of the period, and *Tender Is the Night*'s Nicole Diver does the same.

Sara and Gerald's life were hardly just about appearances. The bedrock of all this fun was their marriage, the solidness of which their friends marveled at. Dos Passos wrote, "The marriage was unshakable. They complemented each other, backed each other up in a way that was absolutely remarkable." The affection they had for each other was always extended to their children.

The family traveled in their boat the *Weatherbird*, which they had built to look like an American clipper and which was named after a Louis Armstrong record that they sealed into its hull. When they went to Pamplona for the bullfights, Hemingway made them do the Charleston in the middle of the street, to the astonishment of the locals. A trip to America included fishing with Papa in Montana and then hanging out with Dorothy Parker and Robert Benchley in Hollywood.

Sadly, it was not to last. In 1929, their son Patrick contracted tuberculosis and was placed in a Swiss sanatorium. When he was well enough, the Murphys went home to New York, where Gerald returned to running Mark Cross, the family business. In 1935, their older son Baoth came down with the measles, which turned into a fatal case of spinal meningitis. Patrick died a year and a half later. While Gerald was able to get Mark Cross out of debt and make it profitable and elegant again, life was not the same. The Murphys found some consolation when their daughter Honoria married and made Sara and Gerald grandparents three times over.

The Murphys truly personified the Spanish proverb Gerald once came across and for which their renowned biography is named: "Living well is the best revenge."

"The Girl of His Dreams"

At seventeen years old, Oona O'Neill, daughter of the famous playwright Eugene, fell madly in love with the most famous film star of all time, Charlie Chaplin. She had come to Hollywood to test her luck as an actress after dabbling in summer stock and was sent by her agent to audition for a role in a film Chaplin was planning to make called *Shadow and Substance*. Chaplin took one look at the dark beauty, and, after determining she was too young for the role, signed her up anyway.

It was a difficult time in the fifty-four-year-old Chaplin's life. A former paramour, Joan Barry, became obsessed with him and broke into his house with a gun threatening to kill herself. Although she was arrested by the police, she returned some months later declaring she was pregnant by Chaplin and asking for money. When he refused to pay her off because he knew the charges to be untrue, she filed a paternity suit against him. Chaplin was also brought up on charges of transporting Barry across state lines with the intent of having sexual relations with her because he had paid for her train ticket. Naturally, the press had a field day. Chaplin was found not guilty and four months after the birth of Barry's baby, blood tests determined conclusively that Chaplin could not be the father.

Oona stood by him, as she would do time and again, as he withstood the circus of the trial and suit. After she

had turned eighteen, the couple married in a private ceremony in a small village outside Santa Barbara on June 15,
1943. They remained hidden away on a six-week honeymoon in the beautiful town, surprisingly undisturbed by
the media.

Oona gave birth to their first child, Geraldine, which
added to her husband's happiness at home. A subsequent
suit was brought against Chaplin by the state of California, demanding child support for the Barry child even
though it had been proved she was not his daughter.
Chaplin was so sure that the scientific evidence from the
first trial would acquit him that he didn't hire a heavy-
weight criminal attorney, fearing that doing so would
make him look guilty. To his shock, after the first trial
ended in a hung jury, a second jury found him guilty.
Chaplin was compelled to pay child support for the Barry
child.

The lawsuits had severely tarnished the star's public
image. But they were nothing compared to what the
House Un-American Activities Committee did to him.
Chaplin was subpoenaed to appear before the committee
three times, but each appearance was postponed. The Brit-
ish-born Chaplin, although a United States taxpayer, was
not and did not want to be an American citizen, saying he
was a citizen of the world. A member of Congress called
for his deportation and Chaplin was accused of being a
Communist sympathizer. The damage was done.

Chaplin made another film, *Limelight,* about his
childhood, that he intended to be his best and last film.
After its completion, he decided to hold its premier in
London. With the family—his and Oona's brood now
totaled four—he boarded the *Queen Elizabeth,* filled with

a sense of freedom. Two days later, the shipboard radio brought unbelievable news: The attorney general had denied him the right to reenter the United States and ordered him held if he tried to do so.

He was slightly vindicated by the warm reception he received in England, and the Chaplins soon realized that they would be making their home there. One obstacle remained: Nearly all of Chaplin's assets were in a safe-deposit box in Hollywood. Since Chaplin would not be able to get to it, Oona would have to go. This was the most terrifying moment in the couple's marriage. They both feared that somehow the government would discover the purpose of the visit and prevent Oona from leaving the country again. For a mother of four young children and a devoted wife, Oona was taking an enormous but necessary risk.

After Oona returned, the Chaplins decided to move to Switzerland for financial reasons. They bought a large house at Vevey, where they lived for the rest of their lives. Charlie took great pride in decorating the house and designing some of the furniture himself. He went on to make another film, his eightieth—he could not help but work—but more and more was a family man. At seventy-two, he became a father for the eighth and last time with Oona, to another son.

After all the years of success and then the crushing disappointment, Chaplin was often asked what was the secret to his happiness. He always answered that it was Oona.

"I love my wife and she loves me. That is why we are so happy," Chaplin told an interviewer in his seventieth year.

One of Oona's best friends from childhood, Carol Matthau, wrote of Chaplin, "He loved women, but more than life he loved Oona. I can't think of any other man who married the girl of his dreams."

Laura

Like Dante, the Italian poet Petrarch was enamored of a young woman who served as his muse. But in Petrarch's case, the woman in question, Laura, turned his whole life around. Indeed, Petrarch would no doubt be unknown today had he not discovered her.

Born Francesco Petrarca in 1304, he studied law in Avignon, France, at the urging of his father, though his ambition was to write. On Good Friday, 1327, at the Church of St. Claire, Petrarch first laid eyes on Laura, and immediately he knew he had found his inspiration. While little is known of Laura's identity, it is quite clear that Petrarch was madly in love with her. It was a love that was never to be requited, but for the poet that was not necessary; just a smile from her was enough to bring him boundless happiness.

Petrarch composed hundreds of poems about his beloved, perfecting the sonnet form to sing of her loveliness. Although Laura died in 1348, a victim of the black plague, Petrarch continued to write poems about her. Eventually over 350 of these poems were collected into a book, *Canzoniere*, whose publication brought Petrarch international fame; his poems were translated throughout Europe, and his sonnets have served as models for poets of several countries, including Shakespeare.

The book is also a testament to Petrarch's great love. Not only are these sonnets poetic jewels, they also thrillingly convey their author's ardor. A single example, quoted here in a nineteenth-century translation, can serve to demonstrate the intensity of Petrarch's love—and the marvelous work of art he turned it into.

> Down my cheeks bitter tears incessant rain,
> And my heart struggles with convulsive sighs,
> When, Laura, upon you I turn my eyes,
> For whom the world's allurements I disdain.
> But when I see that gentle smile again,
> That modest, sweet, and tender smile arise,
> It pours on every sense a blest surprise;
> Lost in delight is all my torturing pain.
> Too soon this heavenly transport sinks and
>   dies:
> When all thy soothing charms my fate removes
> At thy departure from my ravish'd view.
> To that sole refuge its firm faith approves
> My spirit from my ravish'd bosom flies,
> And wing'd with fond remembrance follows
>   you.

Faith

If Cathy C. and Jack M. had met the first time they were actually supposed to, instead of twelve years later, chances are that they would not have wound up together. For both Jack and Cathy, their vocations were religious ones, and they needed the years before they finally met to decide how they could be most of service to others.

Jack was a student at Holy Cross College in 1950 and had a close friend, Bob, who was dating a young woman at Trinity College in Washington, D.C. As Bob and Jean got more serious, Jean suggested that Jack take her good friend Cathy on a date. The two women had grown up together and Jean thought that Cathy and Jack had a great deal in common. A date was arranged for Easter vacation, 1951.

Unfortunately for Jack, he came down with pneumonia and never met Cathy. Around this same time, he was accepted into a Jesuit seminary with the intention of studying to become a Catholic priest, a course of studies that was to take fourteen years. But after completing seven years of studies, Jack left the seminary in 1958, deciding that the priesthood was not his calling. Certain he could be of service to others in another way, he enrolled in Georgetown Law School and three years later moved to New York City to work at a law firm there. He was living in a small apartment in midtown Manhattan when one evening, in early 1963, Bob and Jean, now married, came over for dinner. Jean mentioned to Jack that Cathy was living just four blocks away and suggested that Jack call her.

While Jack had been wrestling with his future, so too had Cathy been wrestling with hers. She had graduated from Trinity and had taken a job teaching at a private school in Forest Hills. A year later, still uncertain of her calling, she enrolled in the Order of the Sacred Heart, with the intention of becoming a Roman Catholic nun. After fifteen months, she withdrew from the order and returned to teaching at a school on the Lower East Side in New York City. While Cathy too believed hers was a religious vocation, she wanted to take a different route.

Twelve years after they were supposed to meet for the first time, Jack and Cathy finally met and went on their first date. When he arrived at her apartment to pick her up, he noticed that the music from *Oliver* was playing. Over dinner at a little neighborhood restaurant, Jack felt immediately at ease with Cathy, but was disappointed to learn that she was to be leaving for a year's teaching post in England several months later. They dated frequently until Cathy's departure.

In England, when Cathy returned to her rented room at the end of the school day, she listened to the music from *Oliver*, wondering if she would ever see Jack again. Her fears were assuaged because soon she was receiving long letters from him. Their letters to each other were filled with their innermost thoughts, and they began to truly get to know each other through them.

The following August Cathy moved back to New York and resumed teaching on the Lower East Side. By then Jack knew she was the one for him, and over frequent dinners at their favorite restaurant they came to realize the beauty of their friendship. One evening Jack decided he could wait no longer to ask Cathy to be his wife. At their favorite spot as usual, Cathy was enjoying her dinner, but Jack was too nervous to eat. Finally he formally proposed to Cathy, who enthusiastically said yes. Then Jack was able to eat but Cathy could not.

The following June, Cathy and Jack were married by Cathy's brother, a Jesuit priest. Their marriage created a union of two people for whom the faith that had ultimately led them to each other was paramount.

All for Love

Cleopatra was one of the most passionate women in history, as well as a powerful leader who skillfully mixed romance and statecraft. Her actions on behalf of her beloved Egypt included romantic relationships with two consecutive leaders of the Roman Empire, in whose hands lay the fate of her country.

Just eighteen when she ascended the throne, Cleopatra decided Egypt's best hope lay in remaining on good terms with the Roman Empire. When Julius Caesar came to power several years later, he decided to visit Egypt with warships and exact from the queen the fortune he believed was owed to Rome by her late father. Caesar's arrival created chaos across Egypt. In order to meet him, Cleopatra had herself snuck to the Roman leader in a rolled-up carpet. He was soon captivated by her beauty and charm and the two immediately began an affair. Relations between the two empires were quickly smoothed over. After bearing him a child, Cleopatra returned to Italy with him, but after his assassination, returned to Egypt.

Cleopatra's relationship with the Roman leaders was precarious again. A triumvirate of men was appointed to rule the Roman Empire, with Egypt going to Mark Antony. The majority of the rest of the sovereignty went to Octavian Augustus, Caesar's appointed heir. As Caesar had before him, Antony arrived in Egypt to survey his new domain.

Cleopatra knew Antony from her days with Caesar in Rome and was pleased to see him. A man of exceptional physique and noble appearance, he was also intelligent and easygoing. He was married to the beautiful Fulvia, an imposing woman whose position as his consort was recognized through the official tribute of being the first woman to be on a Roman coin. Fulvia had remained in Rome to make sure that Augustus was taking care of Antony's interests.

Cleopatra realized the importance of creating a favorable impression on Antony. She arrived in the city of Tarsus on a gold barge with purple sails and silver oars that dipped in time to the music of flutes, pipes, and lutes. As boys dressed as cupids cooled her with fans, the queen reclined under a golden canopy. A wonderful perfume emanated from the barge and its sweet smell made its way to land and Antony. Cleopatra invited Antony to join her. Upon boarding, he was amazed at the magnificence of the preparations, which included hundreds of lights hung in ingenious patterns.

Dinner proved simply an overture. Cleopatra continued to shower Antony and his officers with riches and gifts. She overwhelmed the Roman leader and soon they were lovers. In Rome, however, tensions between Antony's loyal factions and Augustus had reached a crisis. Antony left Egypt—and a pregnant Cleopatra—for home where he made peace with Augustus. After his wife died suddenly, Antony further secured his reconciliation by marrying Augustus's sister Octavia. Four years later, Antony returned to his true love, Cleopatra, and saw for the first time their twin children, Cleopatra and Alexander.

The peace with Augustus was not to last. It was clear that ultimately there would have to be a war for control between them, with only one man left in power. It was at this turbulent political time that the relationship between Antony and Cleopatra was most intense. As well as bearing Antony another child, Cleopatra showered him with gifts, from ships for his fleets and men for his army to rare jewels and a library containing two hundred thousand scrolls. Once she sent him love letters carved on tablets of crystal and onyx. In return, Antony anointed his lover's feet at a banquet in front of all their guests.

The couple continuously celebrated their love and their positions as rulers of the East and West as if they knew it would not last. Soon Augustus forced Antony's hand and war broke out. Although a brilliant soldier and tactician, Antony was outnumbered and overpowered. With Augustus approaching to take Egypt, Cleopatra and Antony attempted a peaceful end to the conflict by suggesting the queen abdicate and Antony become a private citizen. Augustus ignored their offer and advanced his troops.

Cleopatra would not allow her treasures, for which Augustus was desperate, to be taken by force while she was alive. Gathering together the most valuable of her possessions, she retreated to the mausoleum she had built for herself. An alarmed Augustus sent her messages suggesting she would be treated generously if she surrendered. The next day, Augustus's onslaught began. Antony's men, knowing it was hopeless, bravely tried to defend themselves and Egypt. The battle was over in hours.

Cleopatra barricaded herself inside her mausoleum, accompanied by three aides. A mistaken report arrived to Antony that said she had committed suicide, and Antony took his sword and plunged it into himself. As he lay on the floor dying, Cleopatra's secretary arrived and told Antony that Cleopatra was still alive and was sending for him. Antony's failing body was transported to the mausoleum. Asking her not to be unhappy about all that had happened and to think of the glory they had shared while they had ruled the world, he died in Cleopatra's arms.

Upon hearing of Antony's death, Augustus sent an officer to seize Cleopatra. She grabbed a dagger that she tried to conceal in her dress, but was disarmed. Ecstatic at having captured both the queen and treasure, Augustus agreed to let her arrange the proper burial rites for Antony, but she quickly fell ill and was moved to the palace where Augustus hoped to keep her alive. She would not accept this fate and he knew it. She sent a letter to him requesting to be buried next to Antony. When he received it, he knew she was already dead.

As legend has it, she clasped a snake to her arm and let herself be poisoned. Augustus granted her request, and she and Antony were buried with royal honors in her mausoleum.

Pairs Gymnastics

She was the perfect ten, the poised, lithe little girl from Romania who held audiences spellbound as she tumbled effortlessly across the floor: Nadia Comaneci. At the 1976 Montreal Olympics, the fourteen-year-old caused a gymnastics revolution, scoring seven perfect tens and taking home three gold medals.

Eighteen-year-old Bart Conner was that year's American all-around college champion, and though he didn't qualify for the Montreal games, he watched Nadia's moments of glory from home. They had met for the first time a few months before in New York City, where each had won a silver cup at Madison Square Garden. They had even kissed for a photo, an event that left no lingering impression on either of them. Though they would compete around the world in the years to come, they were not to meet again for thirteen more.

In 1984, Bart saw his Olympic dream come true, winning two gold medals. For the towheaded Midwestern farm boy, patience had paid off: The United States had boycotted the games of 1980 in Russia for which he had been the top contender and at which Nadia had competed and won two more golds. No longer a wonder to the world, the little girl had grown up and filled out. When she retired, Bart's future was just beginning. He signed on as a network television commentator, got endorsements, and opened his own gymnastics academy in his hometown of Norman, Oklahoma.

Then, in 1989, Nadia defected with the aid of a Romanian roofer named Constantin Panait, who led her and six others walking through mud, water, and ice until they reached Hungary. Panait brought her to Florida and began to manage her, soon attempting to dominate her beyond her career. Nadia was terrified of him. It was at that time that Bart saw her on television and grew concerned at how she appeared. Later, he talked his way onto the set of a show Nadia was on and offered his help. "It was a light for me," Nadia said. "I was afraid to tell people I was in trouble, but I was always hoping someone would come and take me away." Bart got her out of Panait's grips and arranged for her to live with a Romanian rugby coach and his family in Montreal. They stayed friends by phone for a year.

They began making appearances together and by the summer of 1991 had fallen in love. "I saw the hard shell drop, [and] a warm, caring woman emerge," Bart said of the woman he described as a "mysterious beauty." Nadia slowly became accustomed to not being used. As their romance blossomed, they parlayed their energy into work. Nadia signed an endorsement deal with Danskin and got fit again. On November 12, 1994, Nadia's birthday, Bart proposed with a 3.3-carat diamond engagement ring.

The two were married in a fairy-tale ceremony in the Romanian Orthodox Church in Bucharest in April 1996. Nadia wore a lace gown covered in ten thousand pearls with a twenty-three-foot train carried by six young Romanian gymnasts. The couple was crowned by the officiating priest as fifteen hundred guests watched and ten thousand onlookers crowded outside the church to get a glimpse of the newlyweds. Later a reception was held at the Presidential Palace.

After the 1996 Atlanta Olympics, Bart and Nadia returned to Norman to prepare for "The Gold Gymnastic Tour," a fifty-five-city world tour in which they will perform together. Together they have created a new sport, pairs gymnastics, which, like pairs skating, is choreographed to music. A combination of theater and athletics, they perform in splendid costumes, the setting lit to match the mood of the music. Each performs individually on the apparatuses and together for the floor routine, demonstrating an athletic performance that seems the perfect symbol of their love.

A Journey of Love

There was always something special about Michael J., and everyone who knew him agreed that the woman he settled down with was going to have to be extraordinary. Six-three, with thick black hair and smiling eyes, the Brooklyn-born veteran police officer, who put himself through law school at night, had risen through the ranks to become a deputy commissioner in the largest police force in the nation. Hardly a typical cop, he was a peace lover who hated to carry a gun; his mind was his best weapon. By his fortieth year, no woman had yet captured his heart.

In 1991, Michael decided to take a trip with three good friends with whom he had white-water rafted the Grand Canyon fifteen years before. The buddies decided that they should visit somewhere totally different, choosing the Himalayas and Nepal, where they would raft the Trisuli River. A friend in California who organized river-rafting trips asked the foursome to transport two large inflatable rafts to Nepal for him for a later trip. They happily obliged and while in the airport in Katmandu the rafts were unloaded and given to them.

From Katmandu, the group was traveling on to Pokhara, but their flight had been delayed by fog. Michael noticed a woman sitting in the airport, writing in a notebook. He was immediately struck by her physical appearance: blond, athletic, and wearing shorts that showed off the long legs on her six-one frame. He saw her looking at him and as the delay for the connecting flight turned into an eight-hour wait, he walked over to her and invited her to have a beer with him at the bar.

Kerry R. turned out to be as lovely a person as she appeared. She was on a yearlong trip around the world from her native Australia, for which she had been saving for years. Kerry and her traveling companion had noticed the four men and had given them an extra once-over because they wanted to see how "expeditionists" dressed. Michael was confused until Kerry explained that from seeing the men's cargo, she and her friend assumed that the men must be in Nepal to climb either K2 or Everest, the two highest mountains in the world. Michael was loath to disappoint her with the truth: They were four guys from New York City "who had trouble crossing the street."

Eventually the fog lifted and Michael and his group and Kerry and her friend took the plane to Pokhara, where they said good-bye. For the next seven days the men made a ten-thousand-foot trek up a shepherd's trail in the Himalayas. They ended the trip "exhausted, bruised, and gaunt" by staying on the mountain's base at a hotel called the Fishtail Lodge, which offered not only amenities they had been lacking for a week but a lake view with the reflection of the Himalayas in the water. The four men were sitting complaining about how difficult the trek had been and how their bodies hurt—and Michael was doing what he had been since they landed in Pokhara, talking about Kerry—when the door to the hotel swung open. A Sherpa entered, accompanied by Kerry and her friend, to show them "how the cozy folks lived." Joining the men for a drink, the women raved on about how amazing their ten-thousand-foot trek had been, blisters and swollen ankles aside. The women had not even stopped the first evening, instead trekking in the dark, while the men had slept. After hearing the Australians were still living in their tent, the four buddies never again mentioned their complaints and that evening took the women out for dinner.

The men went on, making a weeklong trip into the jungle and another week rafting. Each time they would return to Katmandu and see their new friends. Finally, on their last evening, the women took the men out to dinner in appreciation for all the meals the men had bought. The four buddies were staying in a gorgeous hotel, which was a converted rana palace, with fireplaces in the rooms. As usual Kerry and her friend were in a cheap hotel. Michael had bought Kerry a gift and asked her to come to his room to give it to her. Kerry remarked on how magnificent the room was and Michael said hopefully, "Well, you've walked three flights to get to it; you might as well stay." "Sounds like a bloody good idea to me," Kerry answered with a smile.

They left each other the next morning, both wondering if they would ever see each other again. Kerry gave Michael her itinerary for the next nine months, which ended with a stop in New York. He was determined to make sure she didn't forget him, so once back at home, he began to make her tapes of music to listen to on her Walkman, which he sent to the next stops on her trip. One tape consisted of rock love songs on one side, with sentimental songs about missing someone on the other side.

Kerry was thinking about Michael as she continued her travels through Thailand, India, and England, and couldn't wait to see him in New York. On her first night there in his apartment, suffering from jet lag, she woke up at four-thirty in the morning. Michael got up with her and tried to figure out what they could do. It was ten degrees outside, something the Australian Kerry had never experienced before. He decided to bundle them up and take her to the most quintessential New York place he could think of. They stopped and bought hot tea and then he drove them to the base of the Brooklyn Bridge. Together they walked the span in the early-morning darkness and found a bench at the middle. They sat there, huddling together and talking, as the sun came up over the city, turning the tall buildings silver and creating an orange glow on the water.

Over the next two years, Kerry and Michael visited each other and spoke on the phone every week. Finally, Kerry, a nurse by profession, decided to move to New York after being offered a job at a hospital in Brooklyn. Another year passed. Michael bought a ring. Knowing he would ask the question just once in his lifetime, he wanted to make it perfect and waited for a night with a full moon. He had decided to repeat their first day in the city together, only this time at night. After dinner at their favorite French restaurant, Michael suggested they walk across the bridge. Kerry agreed and soon they were sitting on the bench watching the moon rise in the night sky.

"I'm in love with you," Michael said. "I want to spend the rest of my life with you. Would you want to spend it with me?"

"Yes," Kerry answered. Michael took out the ring.

"Will you marry me?" he asked.

"Yes, yes, yes!" Kerry answered.

Layla

The centuries-old Islamic story of the young lovers Laili and Majnun, set into poetry by Ganjavi Nazami, is so beautiful and romantic that it still inspires today: Eric Clapton's famous song "Layla" is based on this true tale.

Laili and Majnun fell in love as schoolchildren, and while their classmates studied they could hardly do more than stare into each other's eyes. They spent wondrous days together until Laili's family took her away to the Naijid Mountains.

In distress, Majnun wandered into the desert searching for her and calling her name thousands of times, but he could not find her. His friends became worried for him, as he could not be shaken from his grief. Not knowing what to do, Majnun's father, Syd Omri, sought counsel from the women of his harem, who told him to seek out Laili's father and ask him to accept his son in marriage to their daughter. When Omri did this, Laili's father, who had heard of Majnun's behavior, told him he would not marry his daughter to a madman.

Syd Omri then traveled by caravan to Mecca with Majnun, where he prayed for his son's salvation from "the bane of love." Majnun disagreed with his father, saying he did not want to be spared his feelings because they gave his life purpose and showed his life to be proof of "the truth and holiness of love." The grieving Syd Omri could not control his son, whom he had confined to his house, but who broke free to return again to the desert.

In her new home, Laili too was disconsolate. She heard about the songs that Majnun sang about her in the desert from members of a nearby harem. Now knowing he still loved her and the state he was in, she wrote to him to let him know she still loved him also. She flung her letter over the terrace of her prison, where a passerby discovered it and brought it to Majnun. As she paced in her garden pondering her fate, she was spotted by a man from Yemen who fell in love with her. Ibn Salam was very wealthy, and when he requested Laili's hand in marriage from her parents, they accepted.

The news of Laili's marriage only made Majnun more wild with desperation, seeking for an answer to the torture he endured. After Laili had been married a year, a traveler brought word to him that she despised her husband and lived only for Majnun. Eventually Laili decided she must see her true love and asked an intermediary to arrange a secret meeting with him, but at the last minute backed out; Majnun was crushed again.

Ibn Salam died a short time later and Laili found herself forced to mourn for two years for a man she didn't love. Happily, she had been freed from her marriage burden and could finally see Majnun. The lovers met, but too much time had passed. The years had taken their toll on Majnun, who could no longer speak, and so he returned to his home in the wild.

Bewildered, Laili's misery overwhelmed her and dashed her hopes for the joy she had expected at being finally reunited. Telling her mother she could no longer continue to live, she asked for permission for Majnun to weep on her grave and for him to know "To thee her heart was given—she died for thee!"

When Majnun was told by Laili's servant that she had died, he went to her tomb. At last he understood how it was that they were meant to be together. He lay on her tomb weeping until he finally succumbed to his own death. To redeem the love that could not exist in life, his body was laid to rest with hers at last.

Hepburn and Tracy

Like most actors' relationships that begin at work, the one between Spencer Tracy and Katharine Hepburn was the product of a magnificent onscreen chemistry that continued to flourish offscreen. The two first met in 1941 when they had both just signed to do *Woman of the Year*. Both already huge Hollywood stars, Hepburn had been wanting to work with Tracy for years.

Hepburn, like many of the characters she played, was fiercely independent and willful. She wore only pants because she hated to wear skirts. Married once, she divorced because she could not stand to take care of her husband's needs, particularly when she had so many of her own.

Tracy, an Irish Catholic, had lived a hard-drinking life during his years in Hollywood. He was married with two children, although he did not live with his family; but because of his Catholicism, he would never divorce his wife. Kate never asked him to.

Upon their first meeting, the five-nine-and-a-half Hepburn looked down at Tracy and said, "I fear I may be too tall for you, Mr. Tracy."

Spencer looked at her and replied, "Don't worry, I'll cut you down to my size."

It was true. Hepburn had finally met a man who could match her wits, intelligence, and superior attitude. And she fell madly in love with him. Movie audiences fell in love with them as well, and they went on to make nine films together, including *Adam's Rib* and *Guess Who's Coming to Dinner*.

In her autobiography, *Me*, Hepburn wrote about why it worked with Tracy:

> It seems to me I discovered what "I love you" really means. It means I put you and your interests and your comfort ahead of my own interests and my own comforts because I love you.
>
> What does this mean?
>
> I love you. What does this mean?
>
> Think.
>
> *LOVE* has nothing to do with what you are expecting to get—only with what you are expecting to give—which is everything.
>
> What you will receive in return varies. But it really has no connection with what you give.

You give because you love and you cannot help giving. If you are very lucky, you may be loved back. That is delicious, but it does not necessarily happen.

It really implies total devotion. And total is all-encompassing—the good of you, the bad of you. I am aware that I must include the bad.

I loved Spencer Tracy. He and his interests and his demands came first.

This was not easy for me because I was definitely a *me me me* person.

It was a unique feeling that I had for S. T. I would have done anything for him. My feelings—how can you describe them?—the door between us was always open. There were no reservations of any kind . . .

People have asked me what it was about Spence that made me stay with him for nearly thirty years. And this is somehow impossible for me to answer. I honestly don't know. I can only say that I could have never left him. He was there—I was his. I wanted him to be happy—safe—comfortable. I liked to wait on him—listen to him—feed him—talk to him—work for him. I tried not to disturb him—irritate him—bother him—worry him—nag him. I struggled to change all the qualities which I felt he didn't like. Some of them which I thought were my best I thought he found irksome. I removed them, squelched them as far as I was able.

When he was sort of toward the end of his life—his last six or seven years—I virtually quit work just to be *there* so that he wouldn't worry or be lonely. I was happy to do this. I painted—I wrote—I was peaceful and hoping that he would live forever.

What was it? I found him totally—totally—total! I really liked him—deep down—and I wanted him to be happy.

Bibliography

BOOKS

Piero Bargellini. *The Little Flowers of Saint Clare*. Translated by Fr. Edmund O'Gorman, O.F.M. Conv. Padua, Italy: Messaggero Editions, N. D.

Richard Barkeley. *The Road to Mayerling*. New York: St. Martin's Press, 1958

Lesley Blanch. *The Wilder Shores of Love*. London: Cox and Wyman, Ltd., 1954

George Burns. *Gracie, A Love Story*. New York: G. P. Putnam's Sons, 1988

Thomas Caldecott Chubb. *Dante and His World*. New York: Little, Brown, 1966

Carole Lynn Corbin. *John Lennon*. New York: Franklin Watts, 1982

Anne Edwards. *A Remarkable Woman: A Biography of Katharine Hepburn*. New York: William Morrow and Company, Inc., 1985

Margot Fonteyn. *Autobiography*. New York: Alfred A. Knopf, 1975

Margaret Foster. *Elizabeth Barrett Browning*. New York: Doubleday, 1988

Wendy Goldberg and Betty Goodwin. *Marry Me! Courtships and Proposals of Legendary Couples*. New York: Fireside, 1994

Michael Grant. *Cleopatra, A Biography*. New York: Dorset Press, 1972

Warren G. Harris. *Gable and Lombard*. New York: Simon and Schuster, 1974

Katharine Hepburn. *Me*. New York: Alfred A. Knopf, 1991

Dorothy Herrmann. *A Gift for Life: Anne Morrow Lindbergh*. New York: Ticknor and Fields, 1992

Charles Higham. *The Duchess: The Secret Life of Windsor*. New York: McGraw-Hill Book Company, 1988

George Hodges. *The Apprenticeship of Washington and Other Sketches of Significant Colonial Personages*. New York: Moffat, Yard and Co., 1909

H. C. Hollway-Calthrop. *Petrarch*. New York: G. P. Putnam & Sons, 1907

Joe Hyams. *Bogart & Bacall: A Love Story*. New York: David McKay Company, Inc., 1975

Robert Lacey. *Grace*. New York: G. P. Putnam, 1994

George R. Marek. *Cosima Wagner*. New York: Harper & Row, 1981

Carol Matthau. *Among the Porcupines*. New York: Turtle Bay Books, 1992

Leonard Mosley. *Lindbergh*. New York: Doubleday & Co., Inc., 1976

Ganjavi Nazami. *Laili and Majnun*. Translated by James Atkinson. London: A. J. Valpy, M. A., 1836

William F. Nolan. *Hammett: A Life at the Edge*. New York: Congdon & Weed, 1983

Amina Okada and M. C. Joshi. *Taj Mahal*. New York: Abbeville Press Publishers, 1993

Petrarch. *The Sonnets, Triumphs, and Other Poems of Petrarch: Now First Completely Translated Into English Verse by Various Hands*. London: George Bell and Sons, 1879

Edvard Radzinsky. *The Last Tsar*. Translated from the Russian by Marian Schwartz. New York: Doubleday, 1992

David Robinson. *Chaplin: His Life and Art*. New York: McGraw-Hill, 1985

Linda Simon. *The Biography of Alice B. Toklas*. Garden City: Doubleday, 1977

Calvin Tompkins. *Living Well Is the Best Revenge*. New York: Viking, 1962

Galina Vishnevskaya. *Galina*. Translated by Guy Daniels. San Diego: Harcourt Brace Jovanovich, 1984

Marjorie Worthington. *The Immortal Lovers, Heloise and Abelard*. Garden City: Doubleday & Co., 1960

MAGAZINES

Wayne Koestenbaum. "Love Among the Ruins." *Vogue*. May 1996

Susan Toepfer, editor. "The Greatest Love Stories of the Century." *People*, February 12, 1996.

Anthony Tommasini. "To Us, to Them, La Vie Bohème!" *The New Yorker*. April 15, 1996.

NEWSPAPERS

Daily News. September 17, 1995; May 19, 1996; June 23, 1996.

New York Post. December 20, 1994; December 23, 1994; February 13, 1996; February 14, 1996.

New York Times. April 5, 1996; July 28, 1996.

Newsday. February 13, 1996; March 24, 1996; May 25, 1993.

The Philadelphia Inquirer. June 23, 1996.

The Washington Post. July 28, 1996.

Acknowledgments

This book would not have happened if not for the brilliant idea of my agent Helen Breitwieser and my editor Jesse Cohen and the support of Nan A. Talese.

For tipping me off to some of the wonderful stories in the book, my thanks to: Marsha von Mueffling Crawford, Michael Daly, Marla Hanson, Byron Hero, Joanna Molloy, Liz Pennisi, David Saltzman, Stephanie Thomas, and Susan Weitz.

For providing information, I am indebted to: A. J. Benza, Polly Draper, Susan Isaacs, Richard Johnson, Michael Muskal, David Saltonstall, and Ellin and Renny Saltzman.

Thank you to the best short-order researchers I could have hoped for: Lauren Sheftell and Alexandra Verhagen.

For their infinite support, I am deeply grateful to Joanie McDonnell and Laurie A. Stevens.

And last, thank you to the romantic people who shared their stories with me.